In Art: America's National Parks

("Enjoying Great Art" Series)

Brought to you by

Deirdre K. Fuller

Other books in the "Enjoying Great Art" Series by Catherine Jaime:
- In Art: Leonardo
- In Art: Turkey
- In Art: New York City
- In Art: Animals
- In Art: Horses
- In Art: Cats
- In Art: Hats
- In Art: Self-Portraits
- In Art: Books
- In Art: Bridges
- In Art: Christmas
- In Art: Lighthouses
- In Art: Food
- In Art: Umbrellas and Parasols

Other books in the "Enjoying Great Art" Series by Deirdre Fuller:
- In Art: U.S. Presidents
- In Art: Art
- In Art: Birds
- In Art: Butterflies
- In Art: Chickens
- In Art: Dogs
- In Art: Farming
- In Art: Pugs

Other National Park projects by Deirdre Fuller
- Waffle's Trip to Big Bend National Park
- The National Parks: Through Our Eyes

www.CreativeLearningConnection.com

We may think of the National Parks as places to go on vacation, or places to learn about our history. But do we think of them as a part of great art?

Here is a picture book for students of all ages...A picture book of the parks in art! Different geography, animals and people...Some that are landscapes of the parks, some that show animals that are an important part of the parks.

Look through these paintings that span more than two hundred years, and notice the similarities and the differences between them...See the colors, the textures, the patterns, and more.

Note to parents:
All of the paintings selected for the books in this series are child-friendly - but we aren't necessarily recommending all of the other paintings by these same artists! If you and your children want to go exploring after this - please exercise caution.

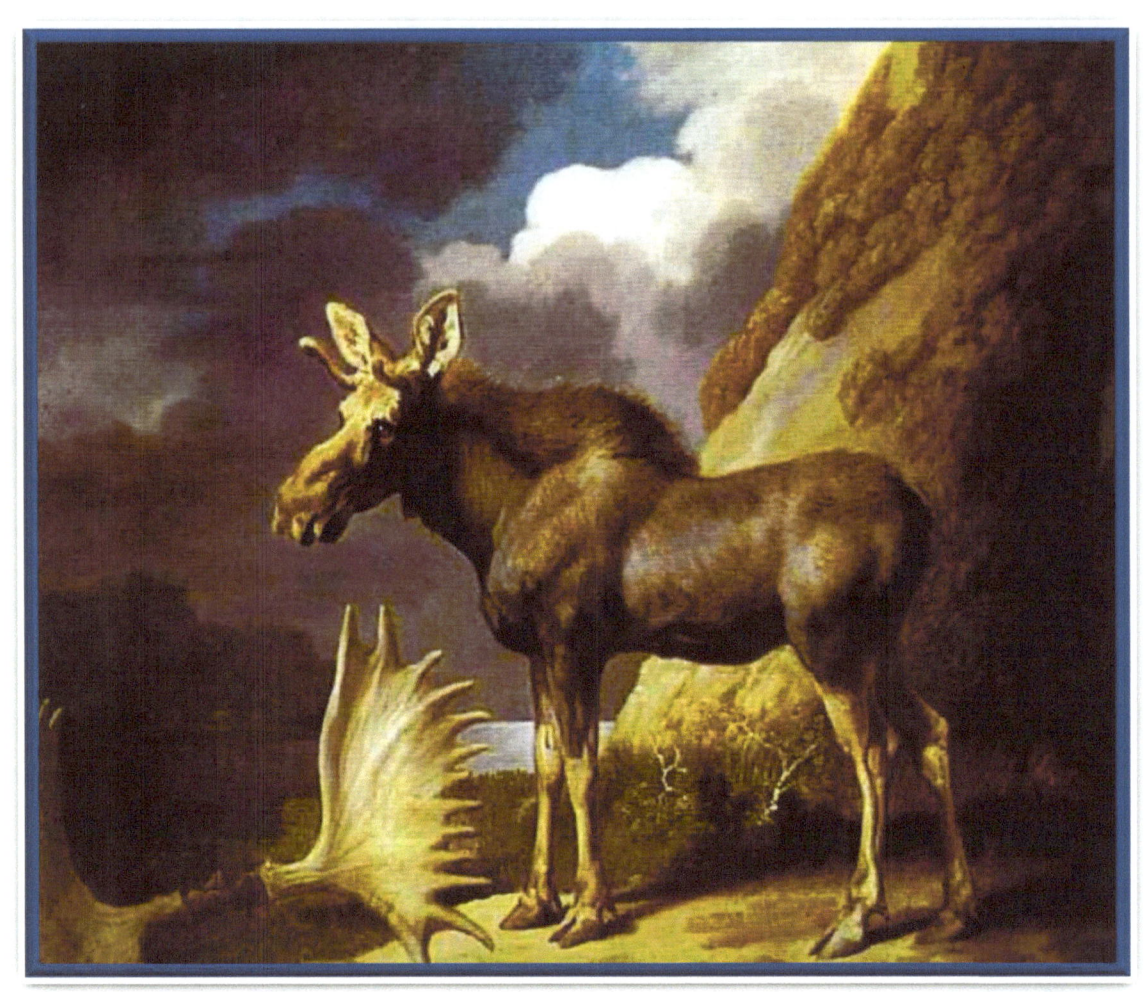

The Moose

George Stubbs, 1776

Rocky Mountain National Park

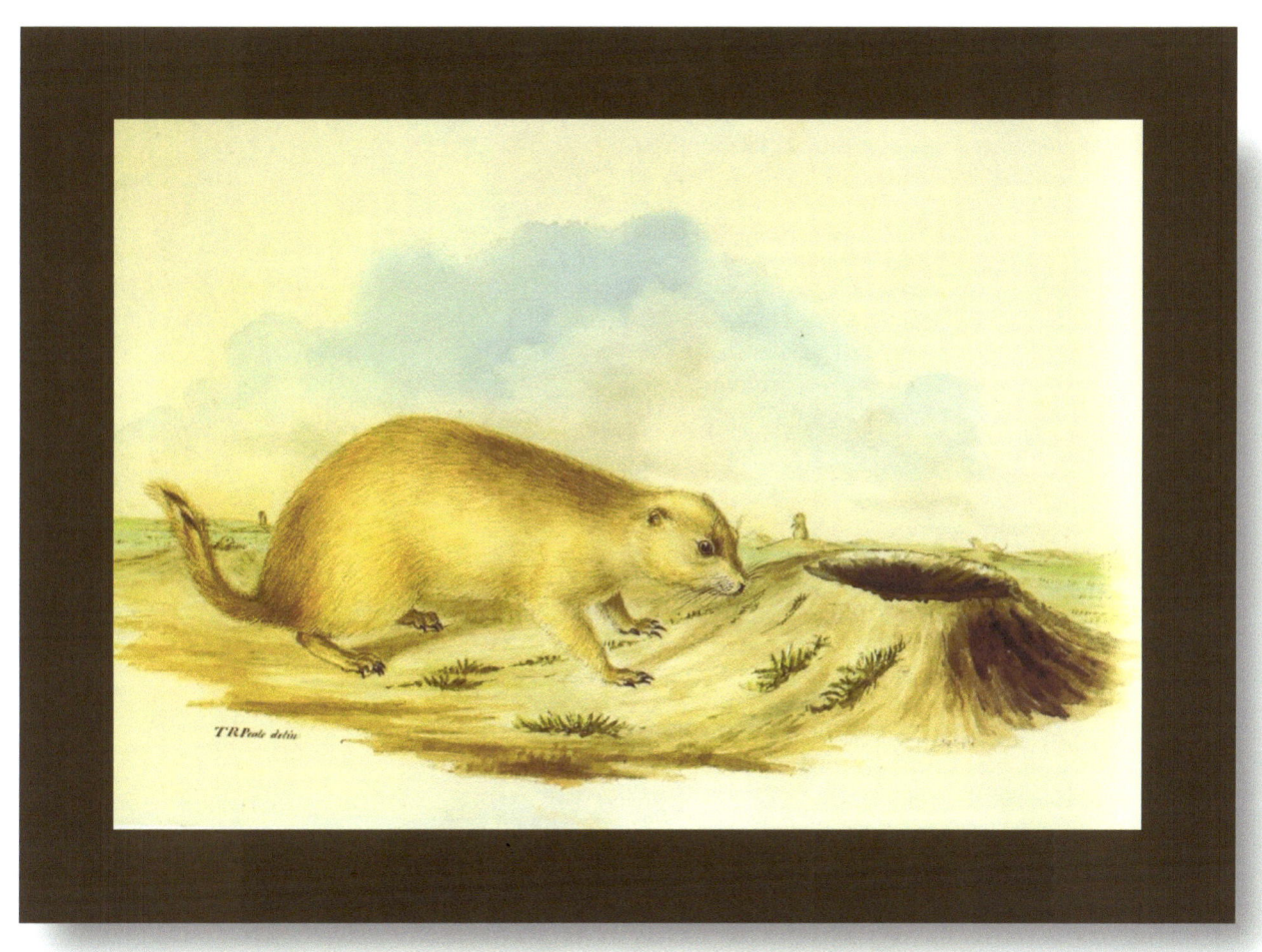

Prairie Dog

Titian Ramsay Peale, 1819-1821

Wind Cave National Park

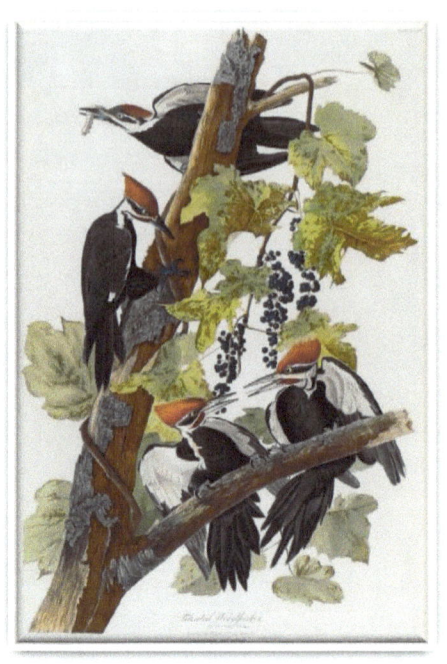

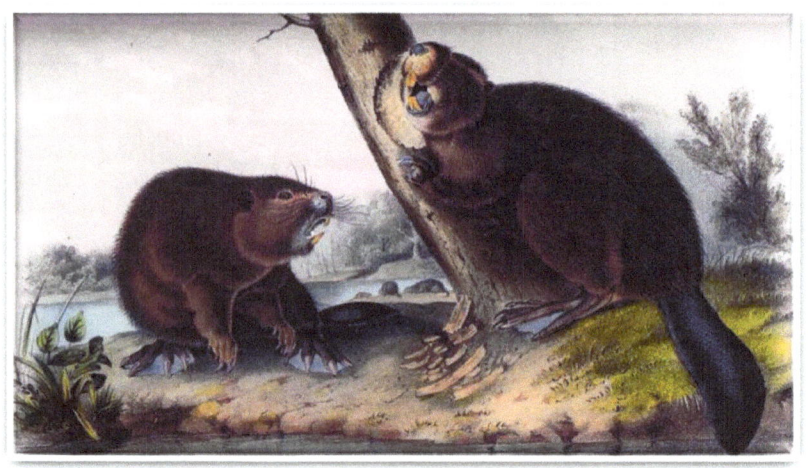

Upper- Pileated Woodpecker

Lower- North American Beaver

Both- James John Audubon,

early 1800s

Appalachian National Scenic Trail

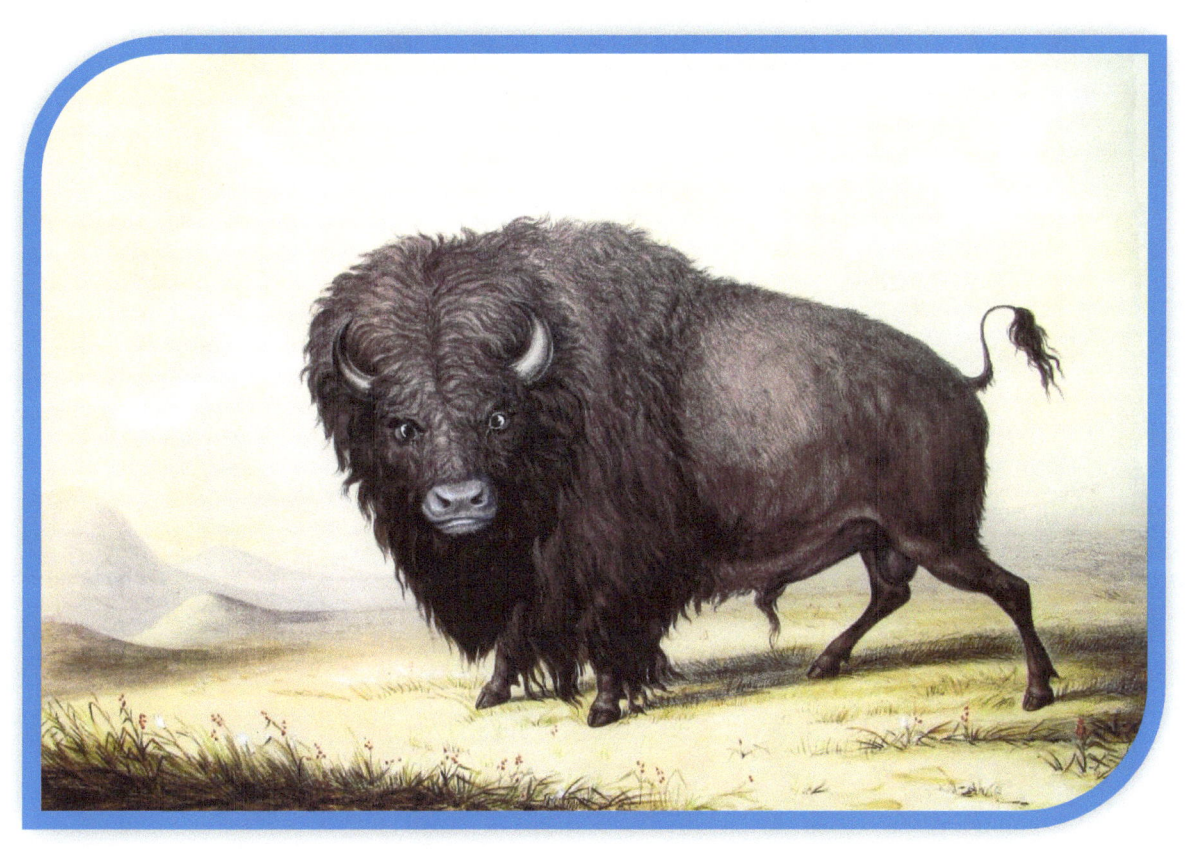

Bull Buffalo

George Catlin, 1846

Theodore Roosevelt National Park

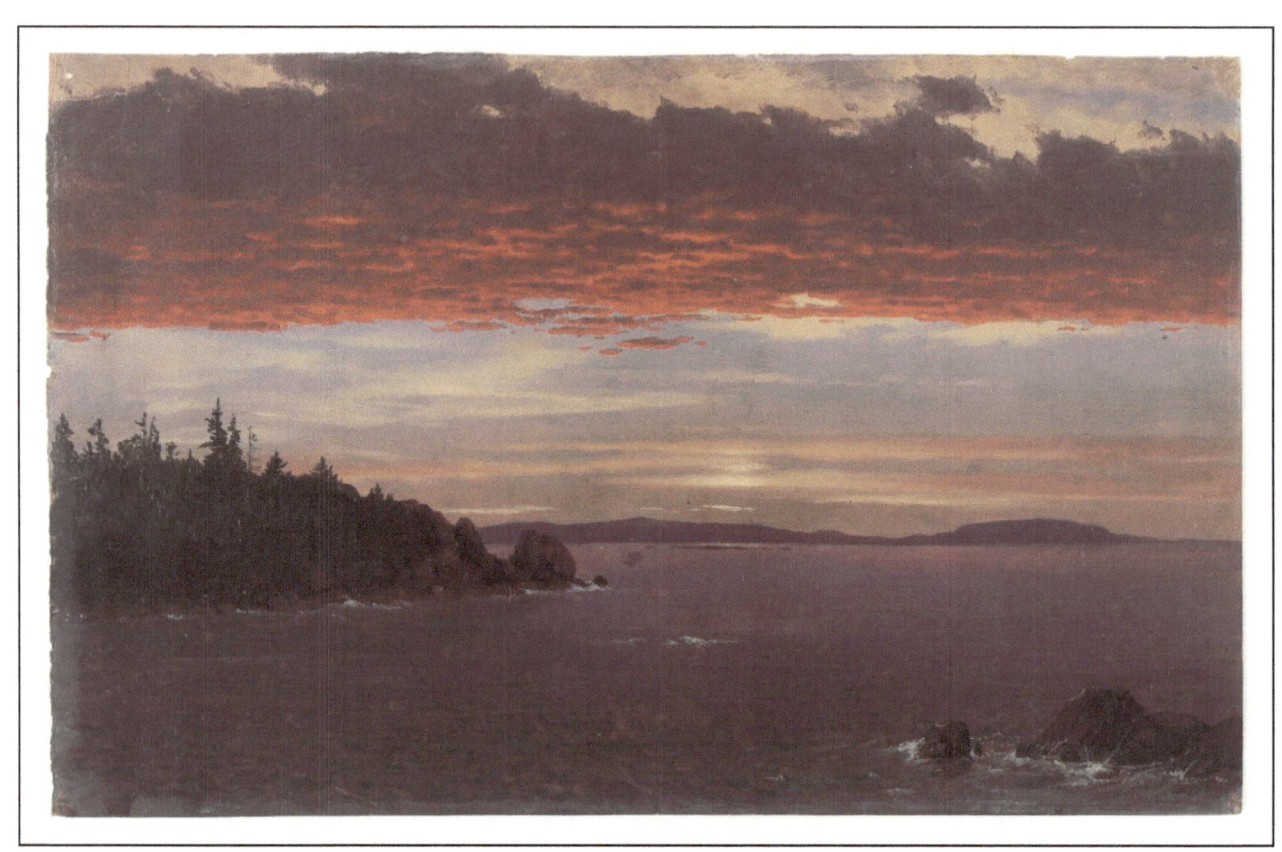

Schoodic Peninsula from Mount Desert at Sunrise

Frederic Edwin Church, 1850-55

Acadia National Park

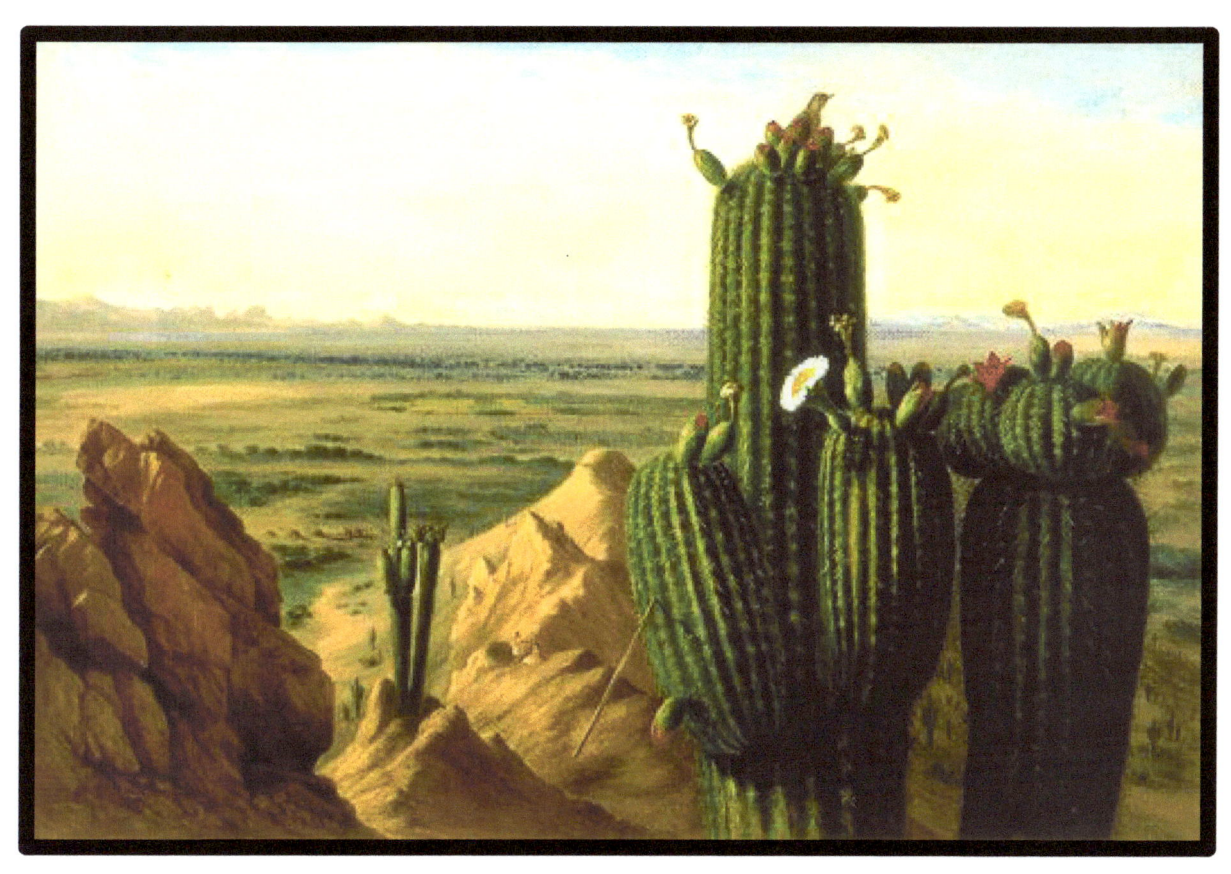

**View from Maricopa Mountain
near the Rio Gila
Henry Cheever Pratt, 1855
Saguaro National Park**

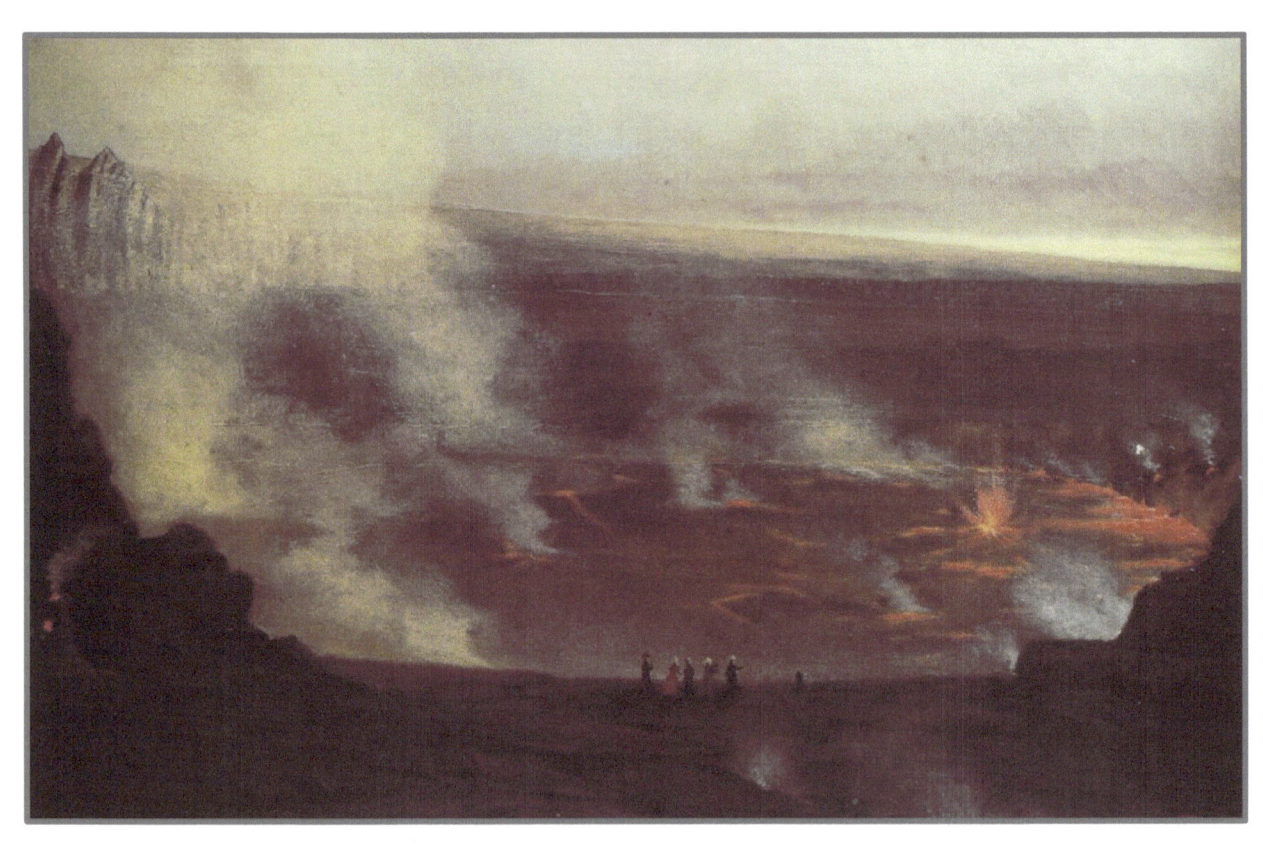

Kilauea Volcano

William Pinkney Toler, 1860s

Hawai'i Volcanoes National Park

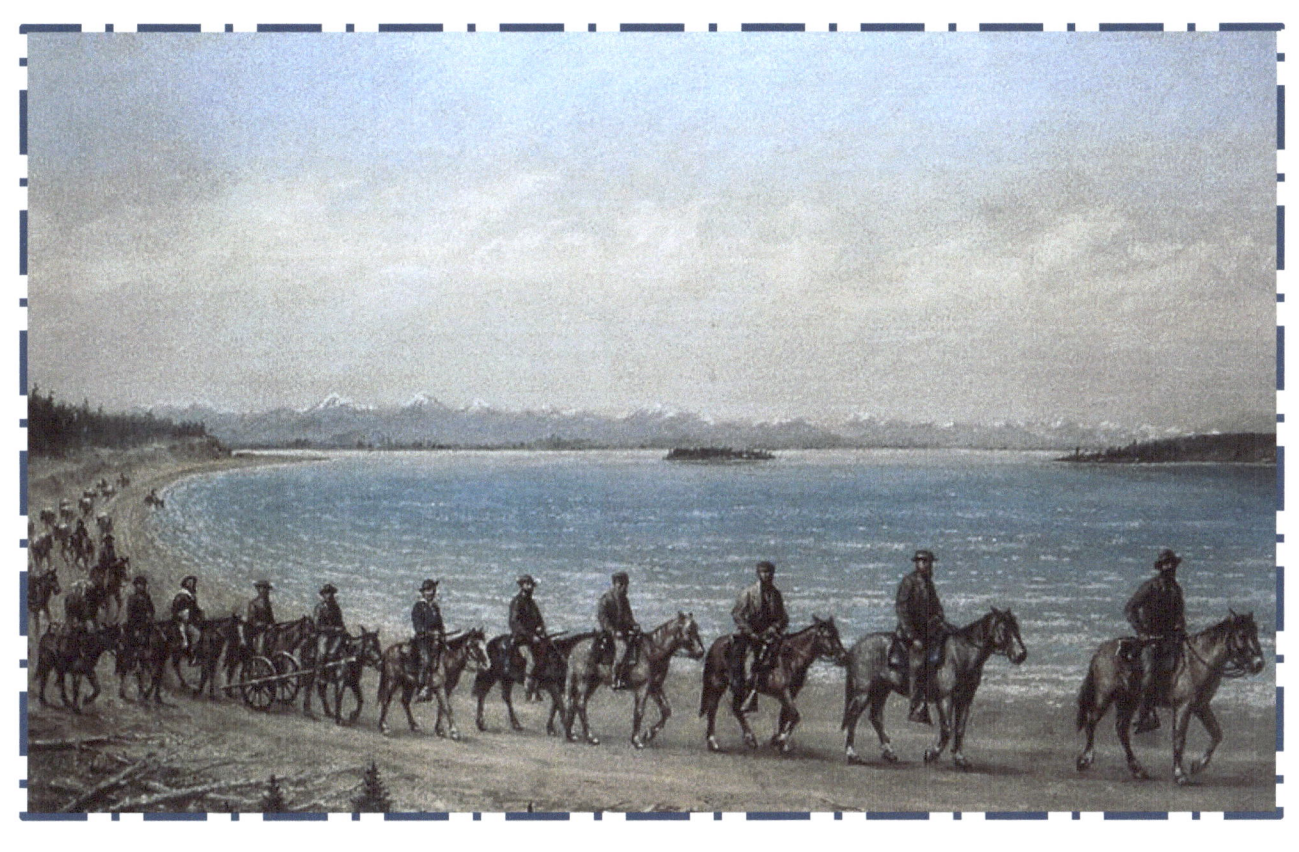

Hayden Expedition

William Henry Jackson, 1871

Yellowstone National Park

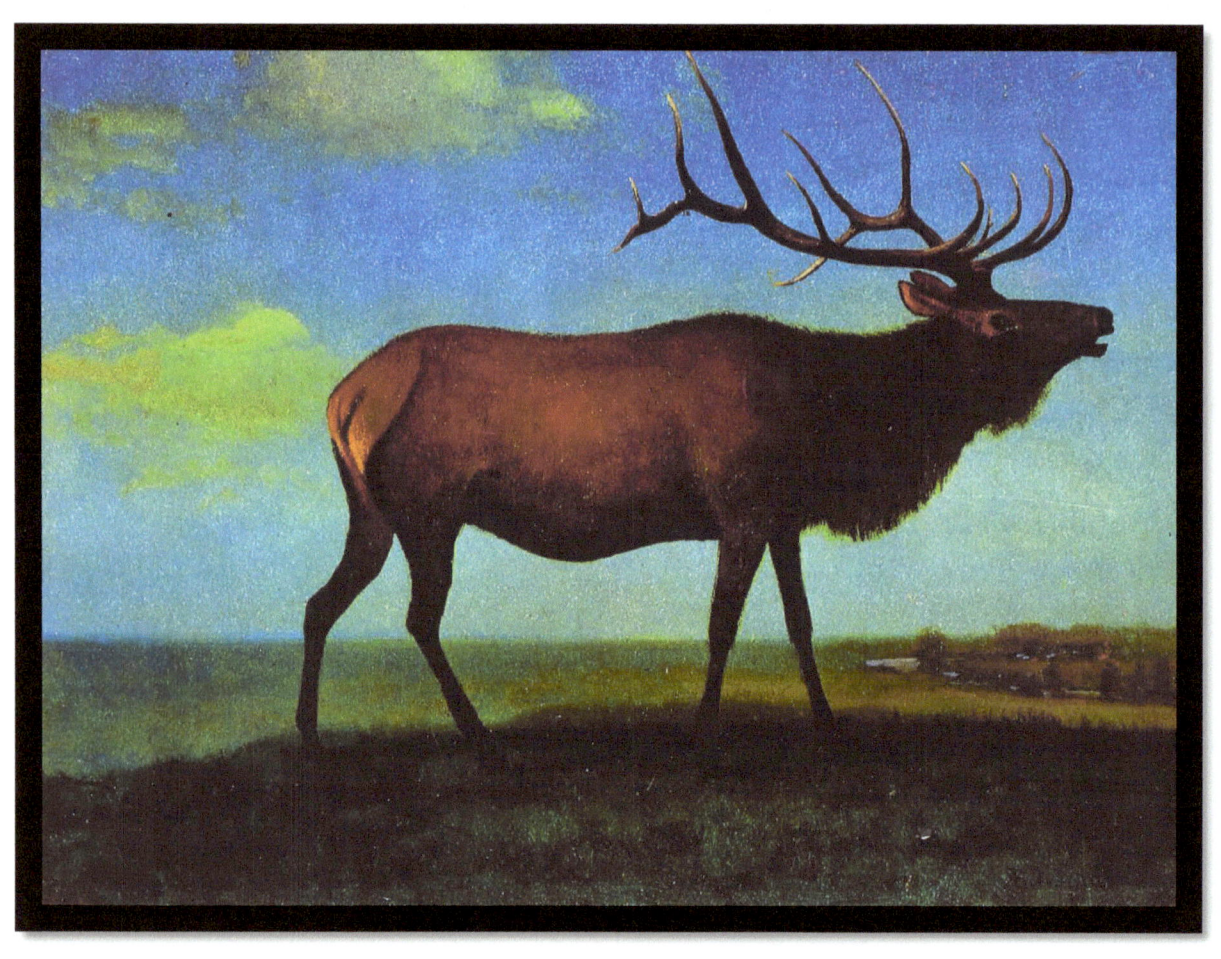

Bull Elk

Albert Bierstadt, c. mid 1800s

Great Smokey Mountains

National Park

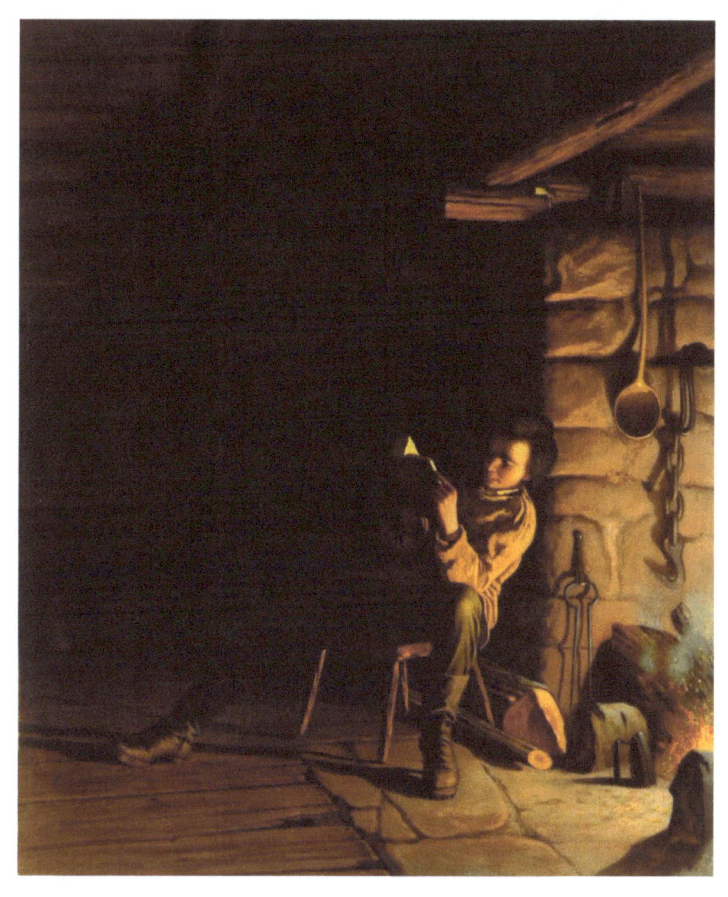

The Boyhood of Lincoln,
an Evening in the Log Hut
Eastman Johnson, 1868
Lincoln Boyhood National Memorial

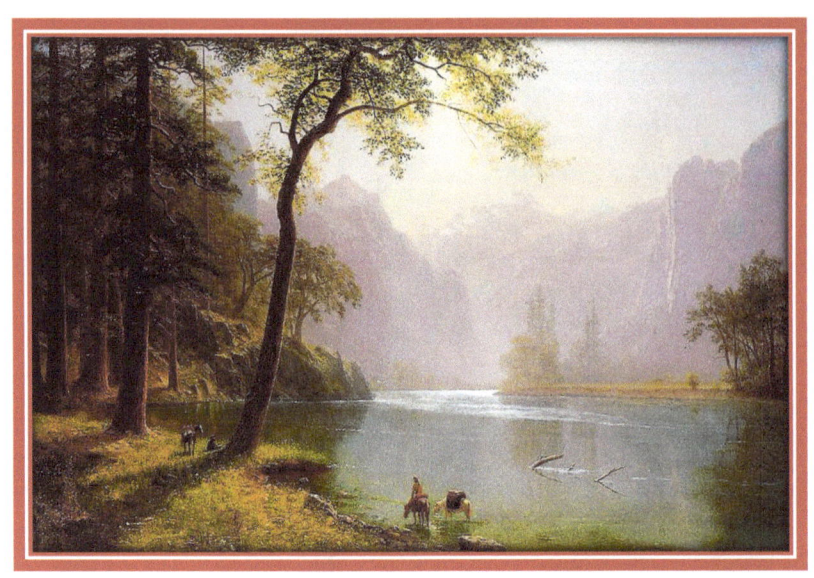

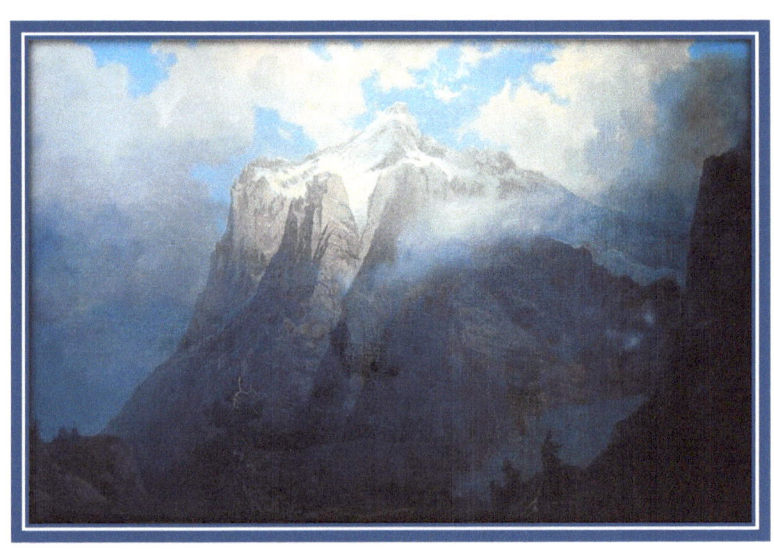

Upper- Kern's River Valley, 1871

Lower- Mount Brewer, 1872

Both- Albert Bierstadt

Both- Sequoia & Kings Canyon

National Park

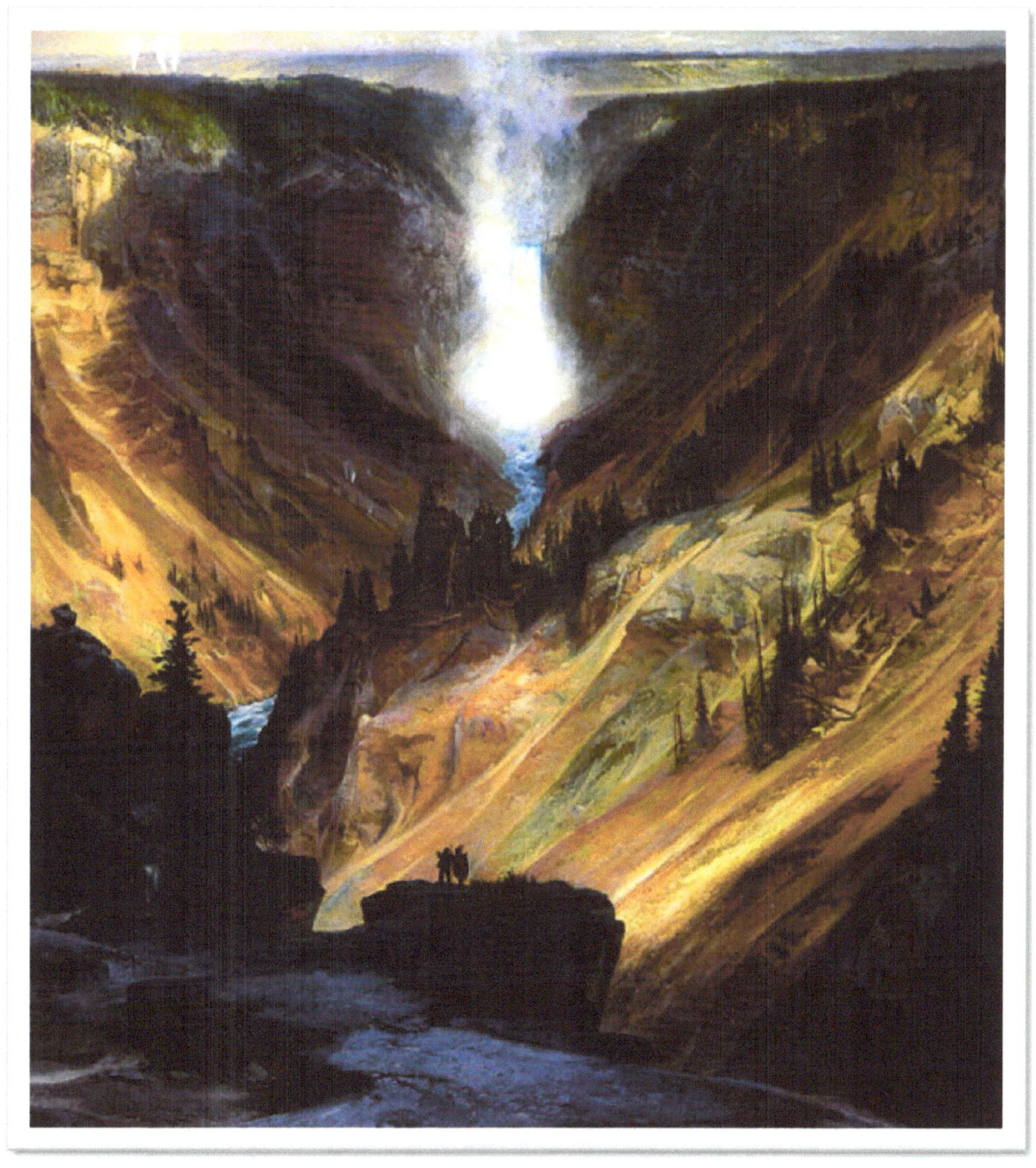

Yellowstone Canyon

Thomas Moran, 1872

Yellowstone National Park

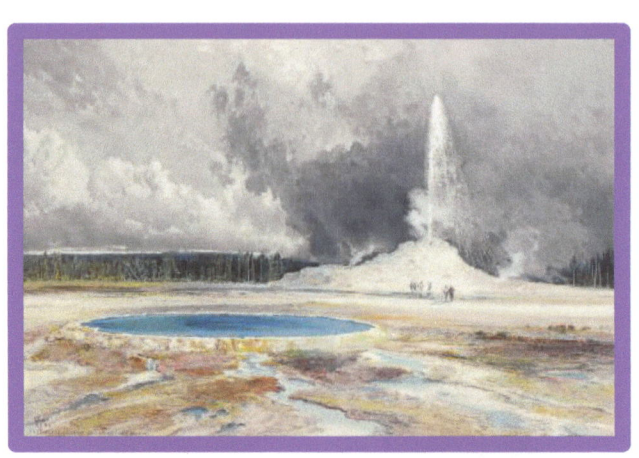

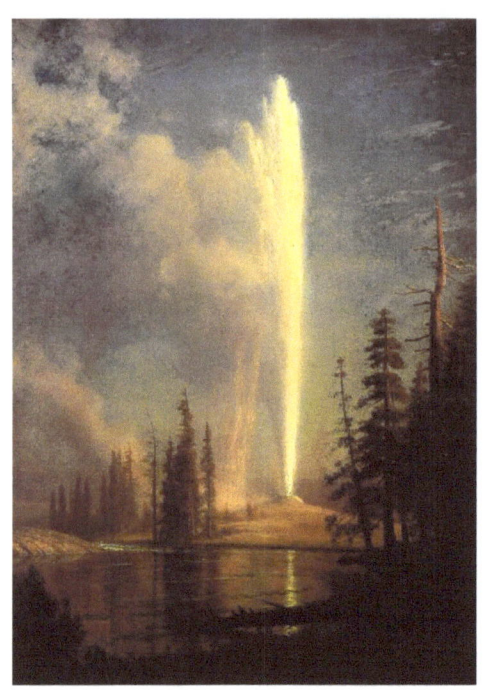

Castle Geyser

Ferdinand Vandeveer, 1874

Old Faithful,

Albert Bierstadt, 1881

Yellowstone National Park

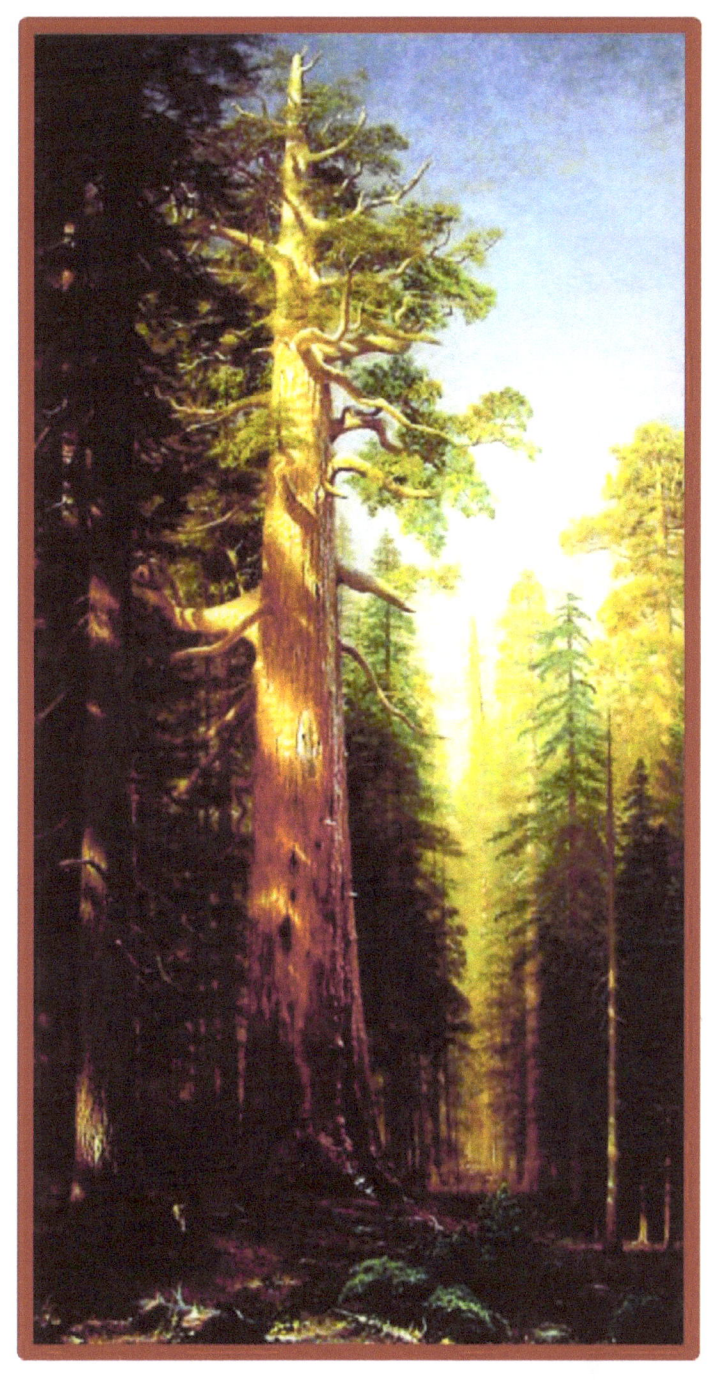

The Great Trees

Albert Bierstadt, 1876

Yosemite National Park

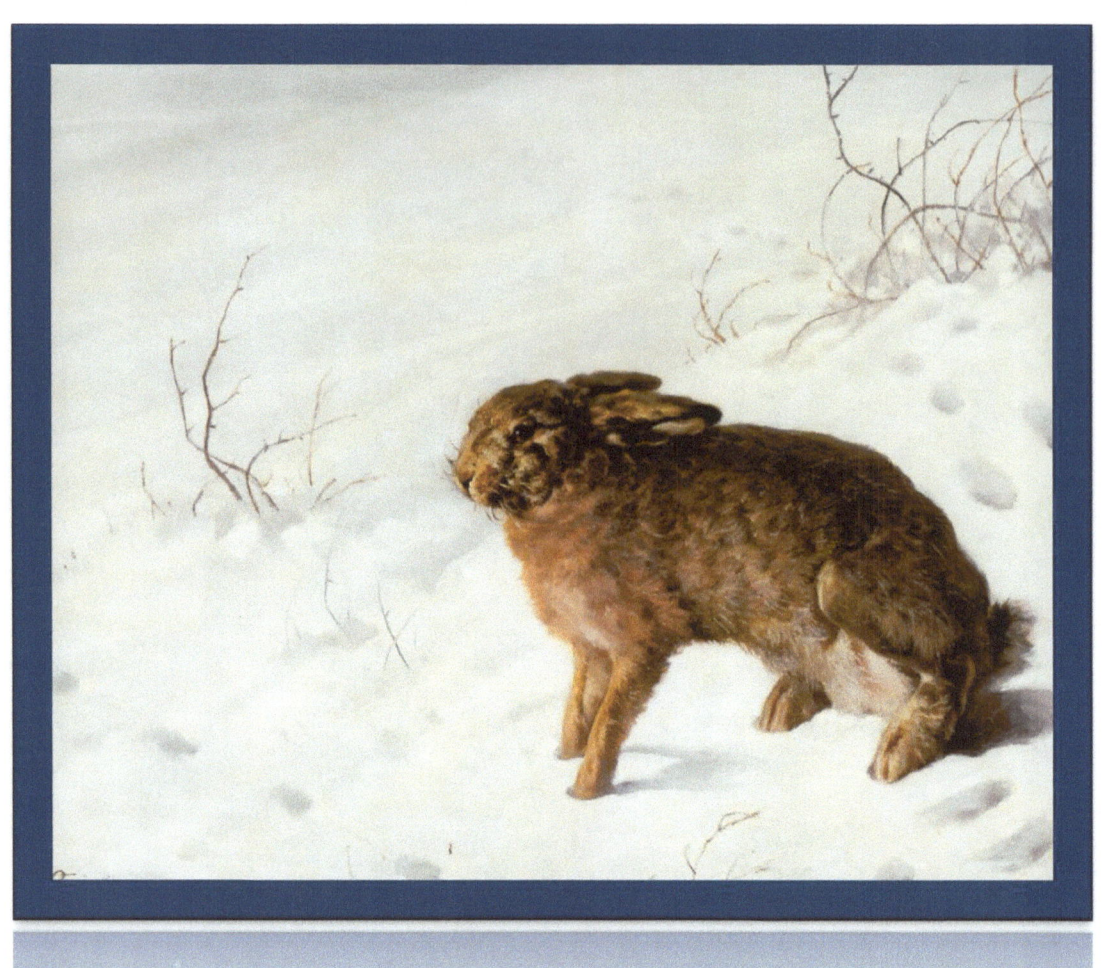

Hare in the Snow

Ferdinand von Rayski, 1875

Denali National Park

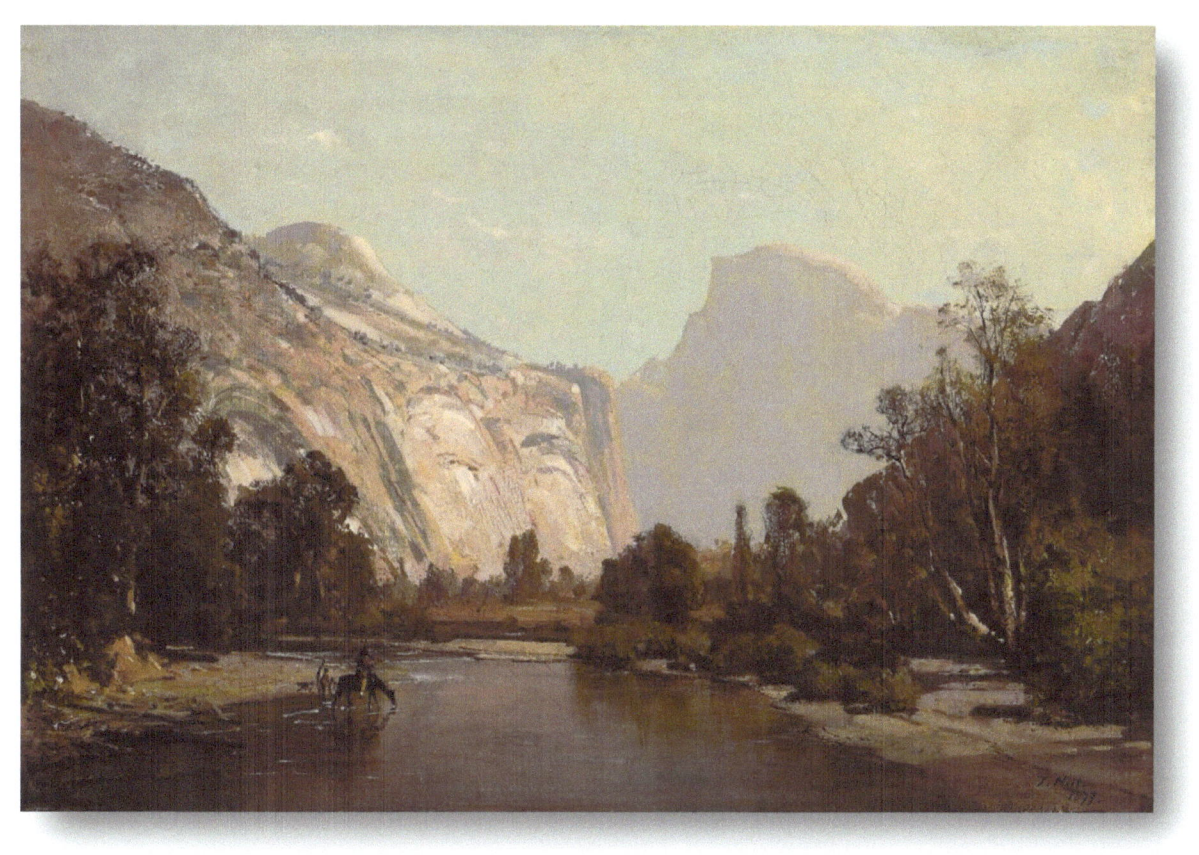

Royal Arches and Domes of Yosemite

Thomas Hill, 1879

Yosemite National Park

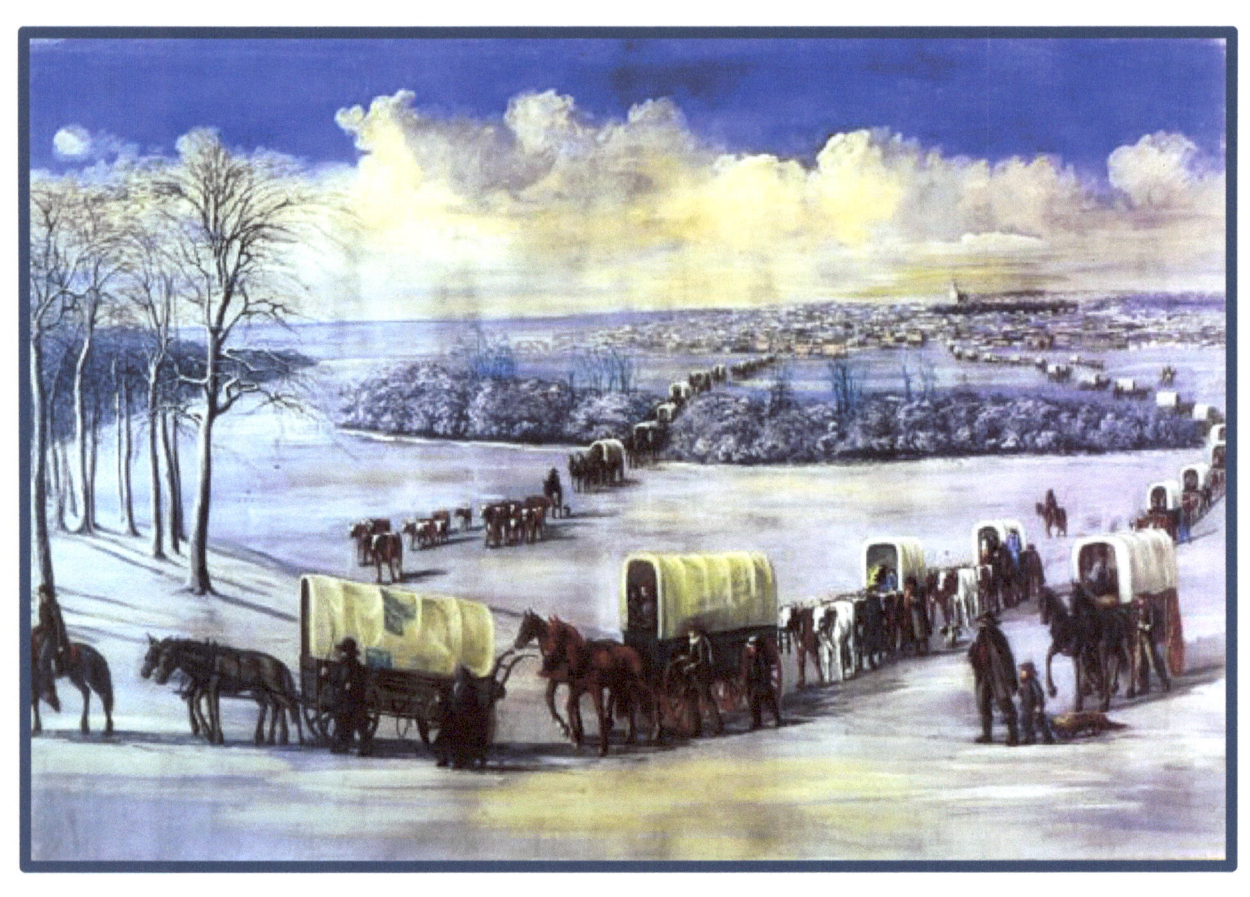

Crossing the Mississippi on the Ice

Carl C. A. Christensen, c. Mid 1800s

California National Historic Trail

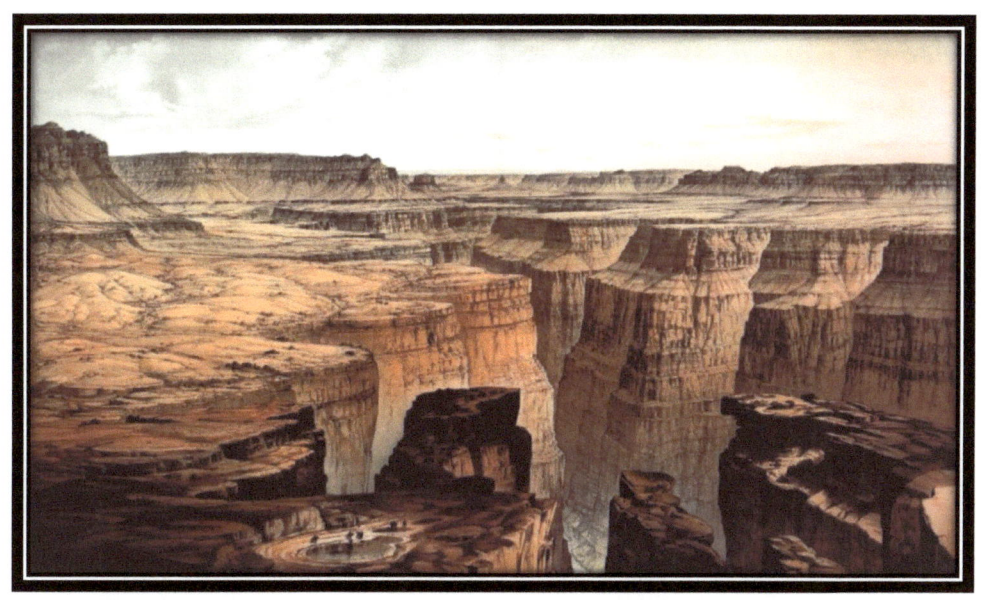

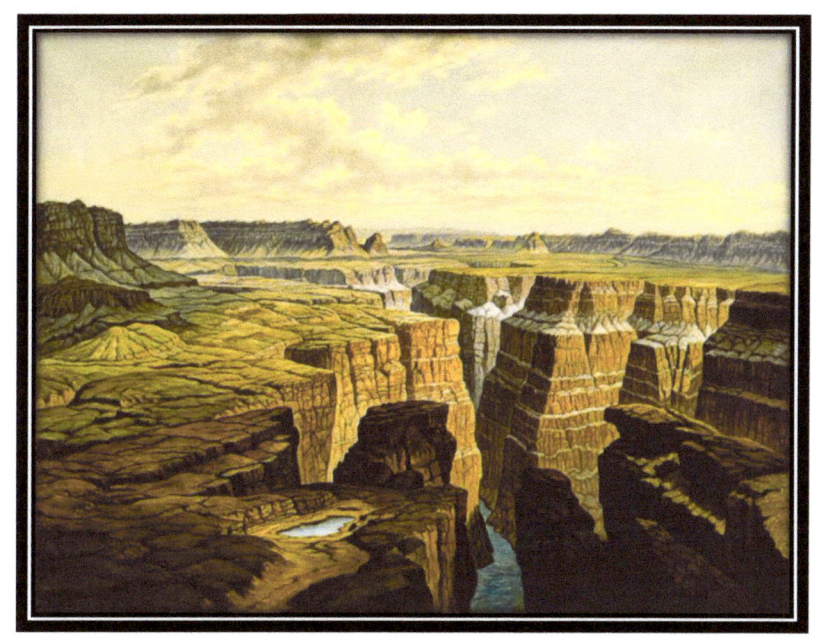

Both- The Grand Canyon at the Foot of the Toroweap-Looking East

Upper- William Henry Holmes 1882

Lower- Hubert Sattler 1800s

Grand Canyon National Park

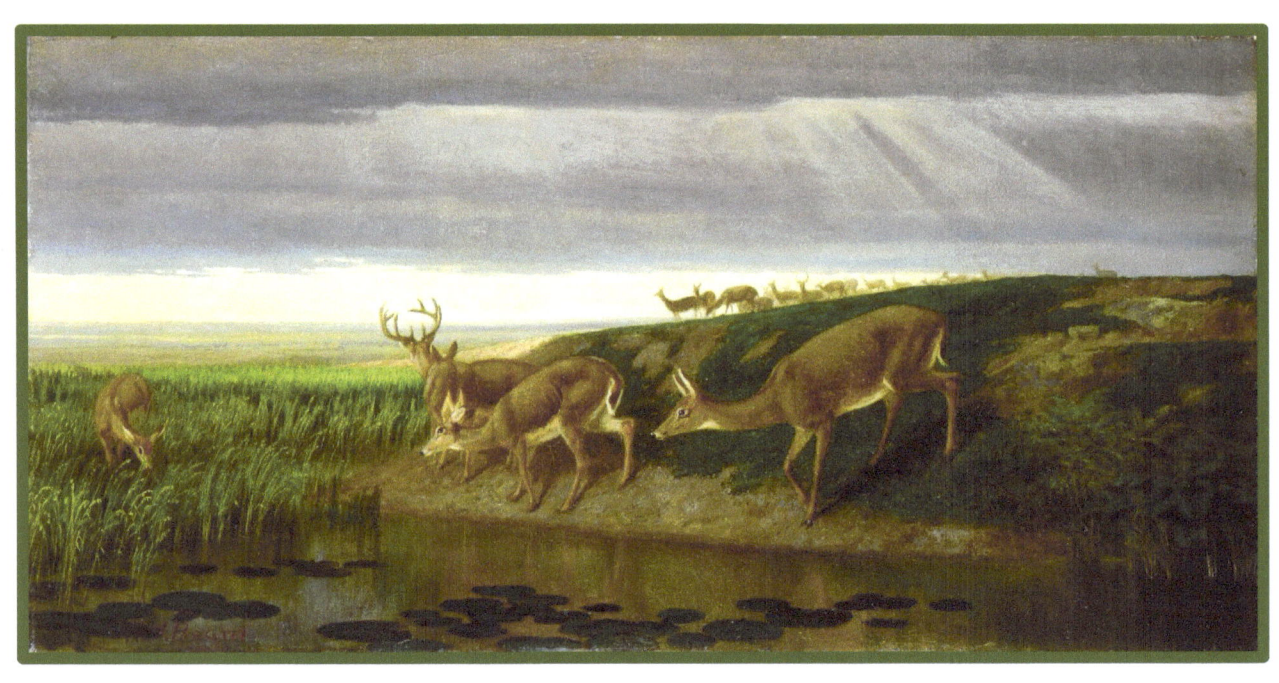

Deer on the Prairie

William Holbrook Beard, 1884

Missouri National Recreational River

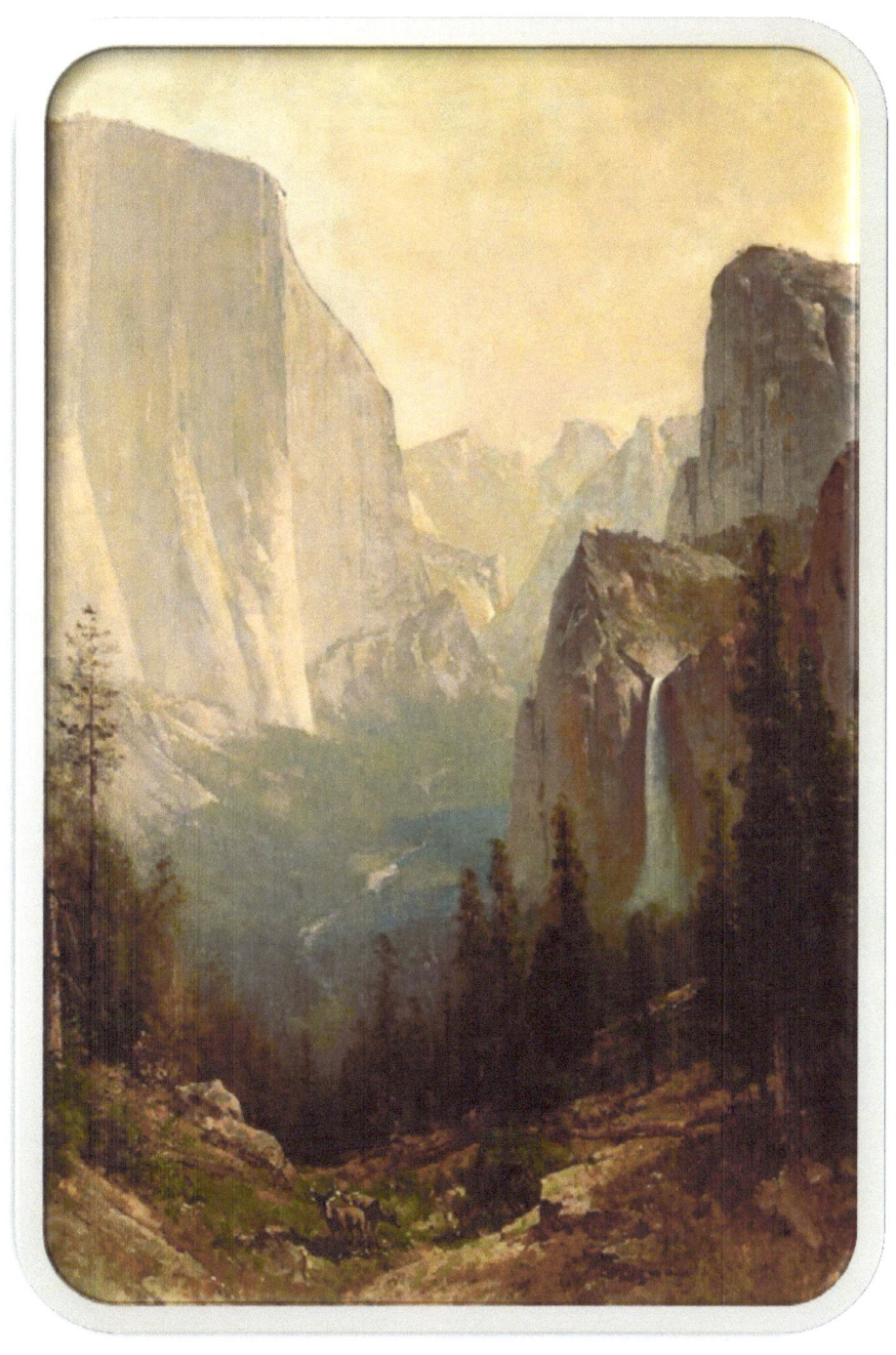

Early Morning Yosemite Valley

Thomas Hill, 1884

Yosemite National Park

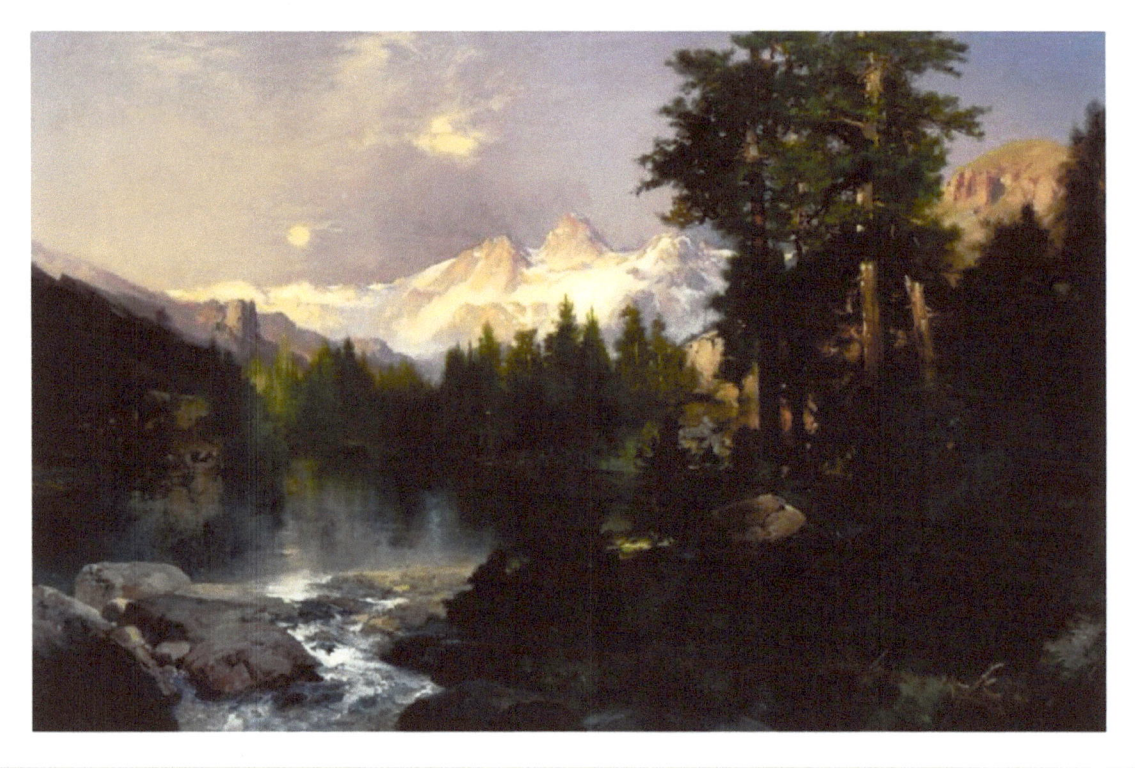

The Three Tetons

Thomas Moran, 1895

Grand Teton National Park

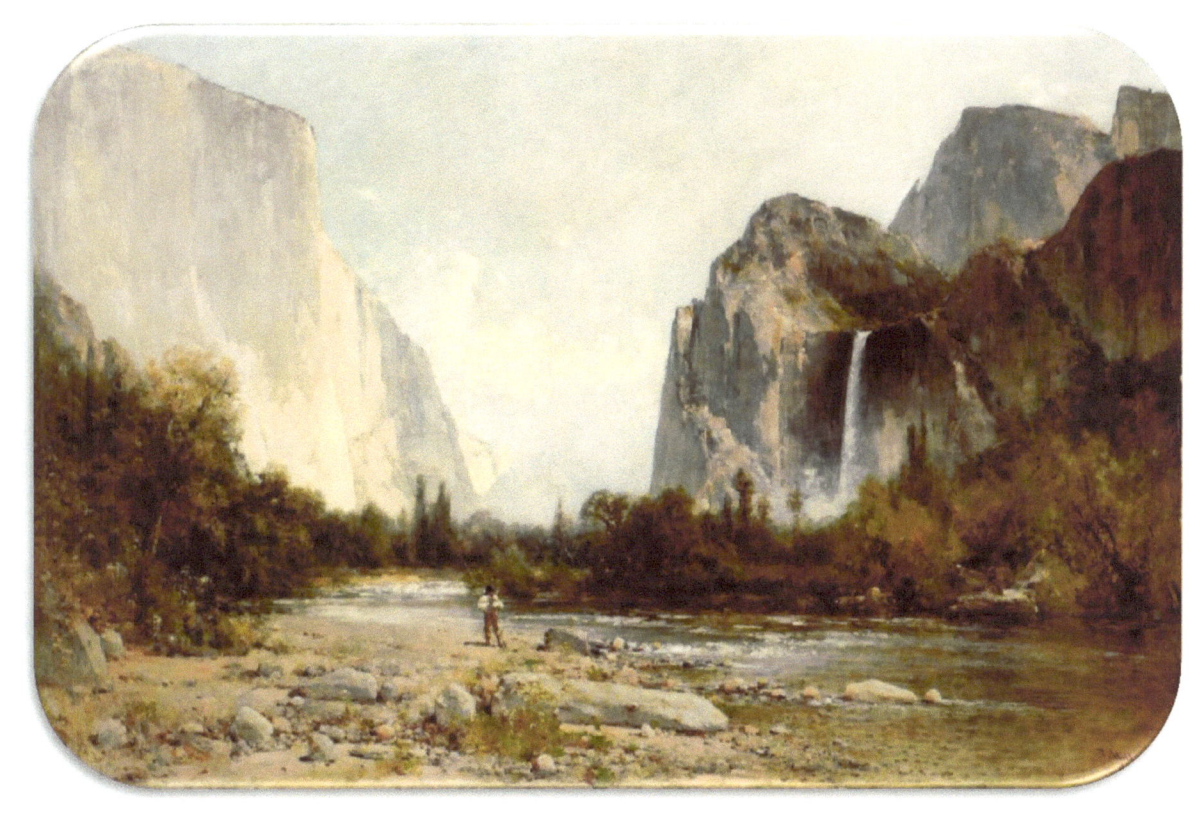

Bridal Veil Falls

Thomas Hill, 1895

Yosemite National Park

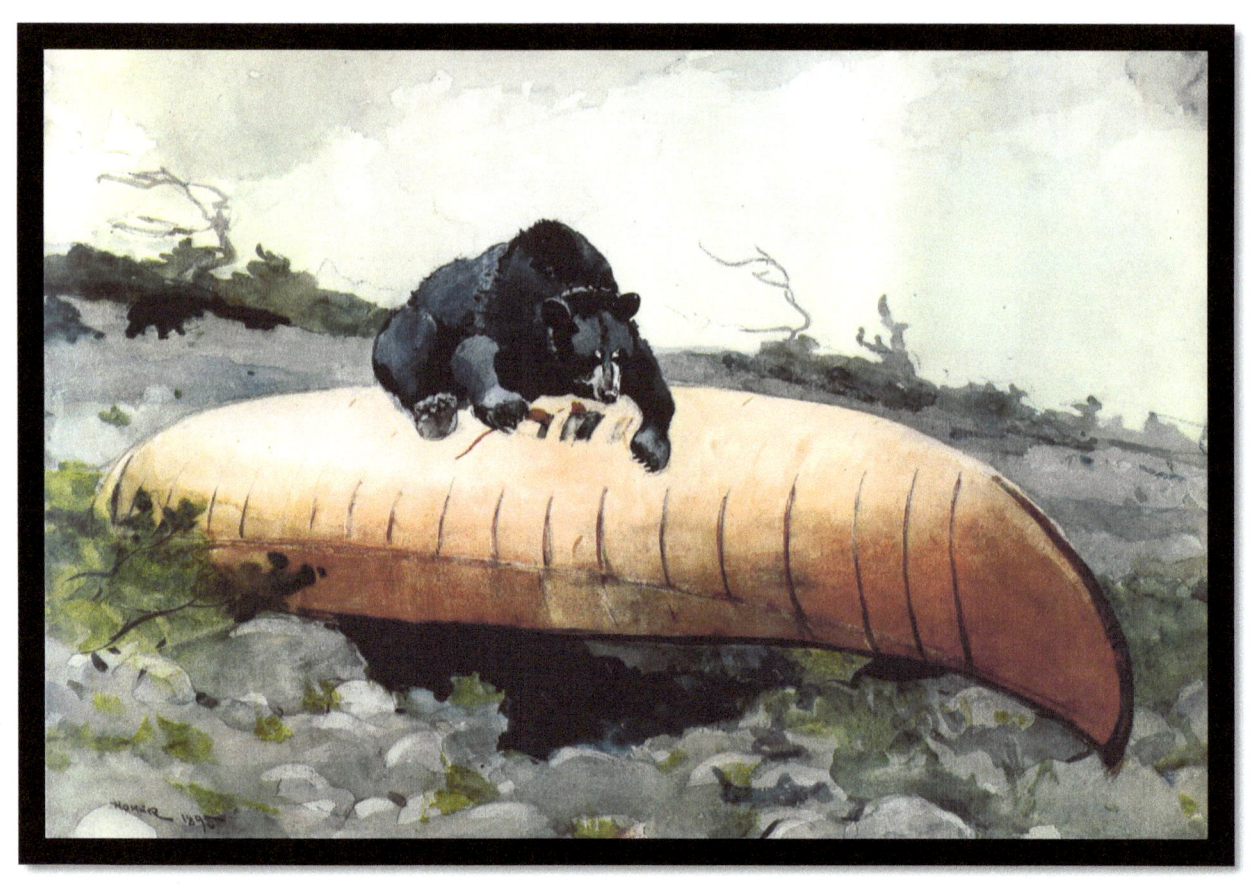

Bear and Canoe

Winslow Homer, 1895

Olympic National Park

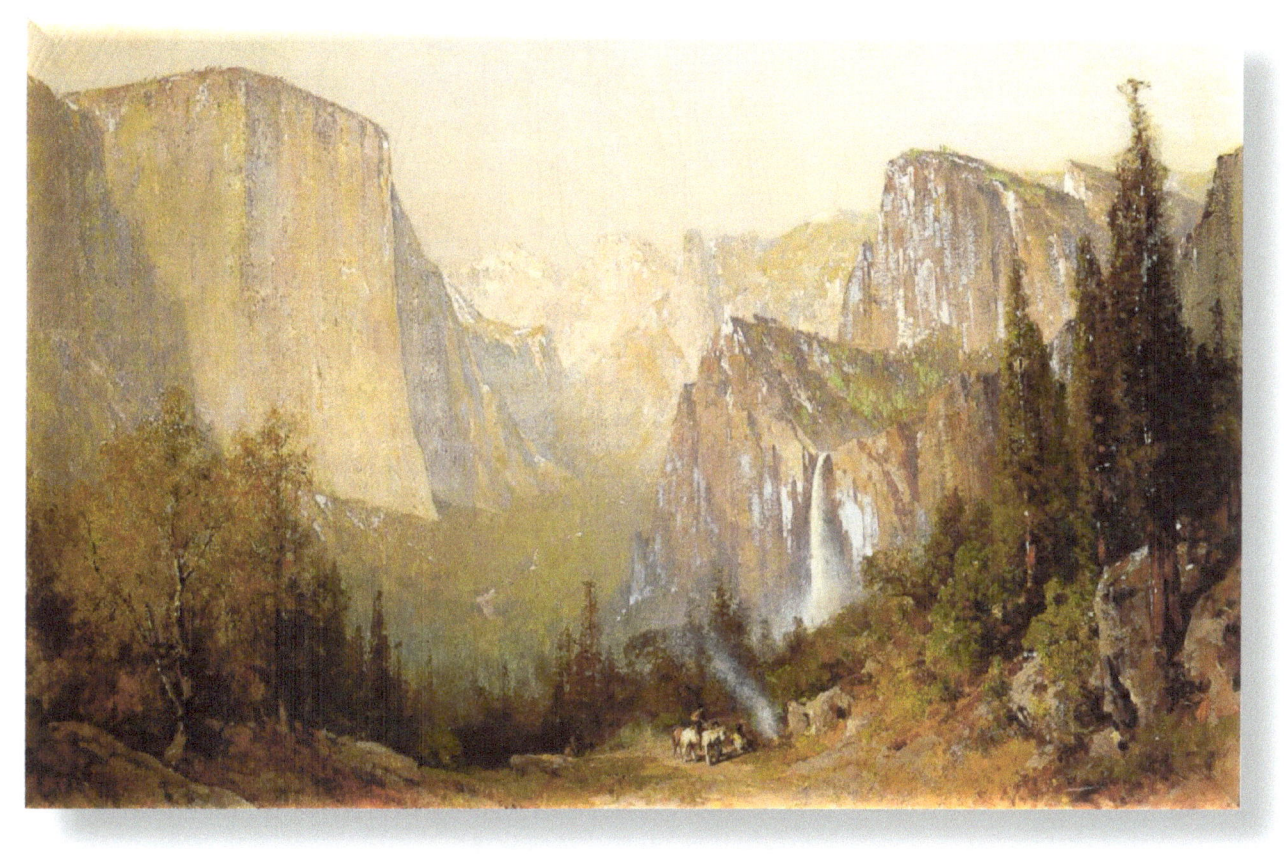

Yosemite Valley

Thomas Hill, 1900

Yosemite National Park

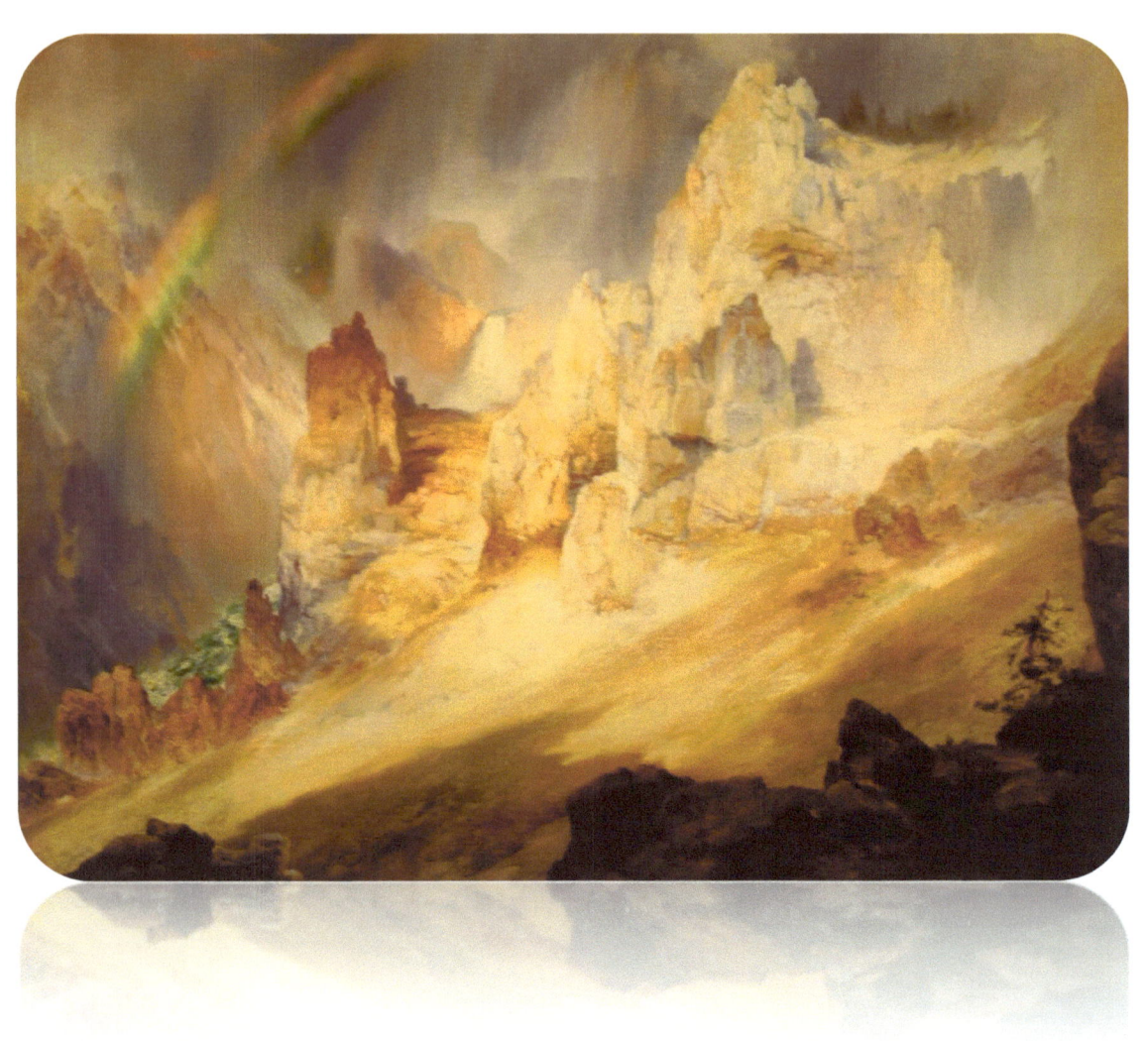

Rainbow over the

Grand Canyon of the Yellowstone

Thomas Moran, 1900

Yellowstone National Park

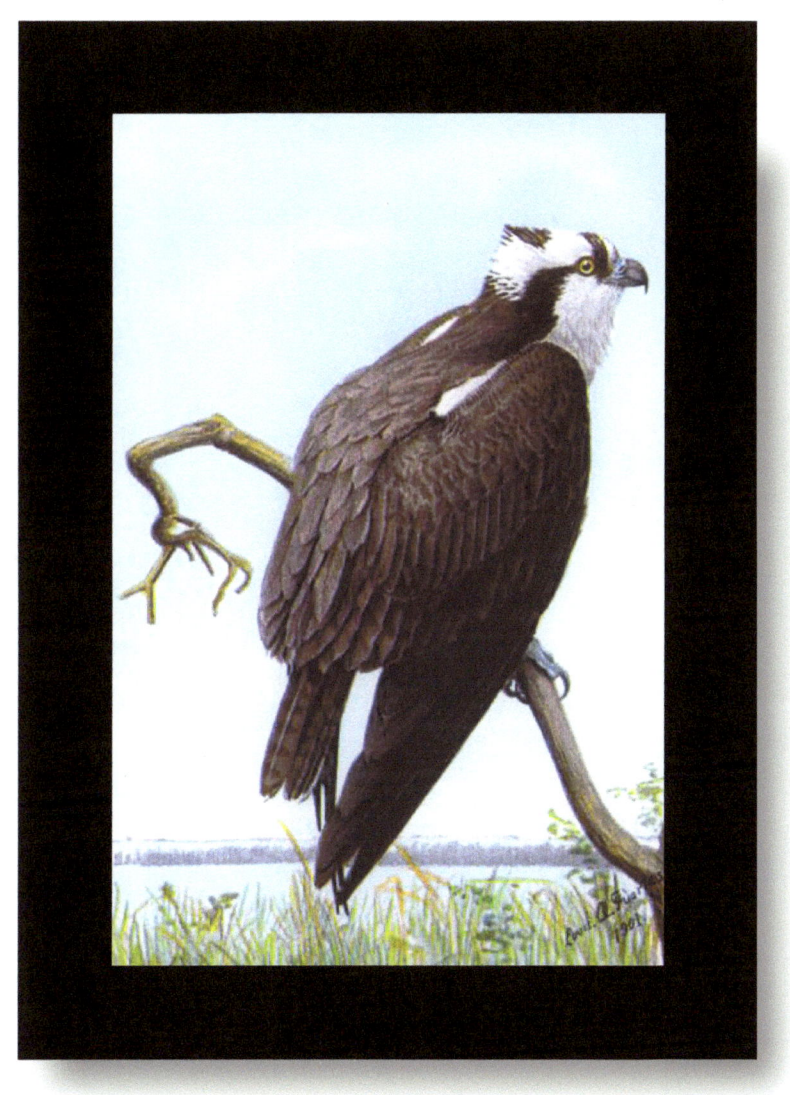

Osprey

Louis Agassiz Fuertes, 1901

Gulf Islands National Seashore

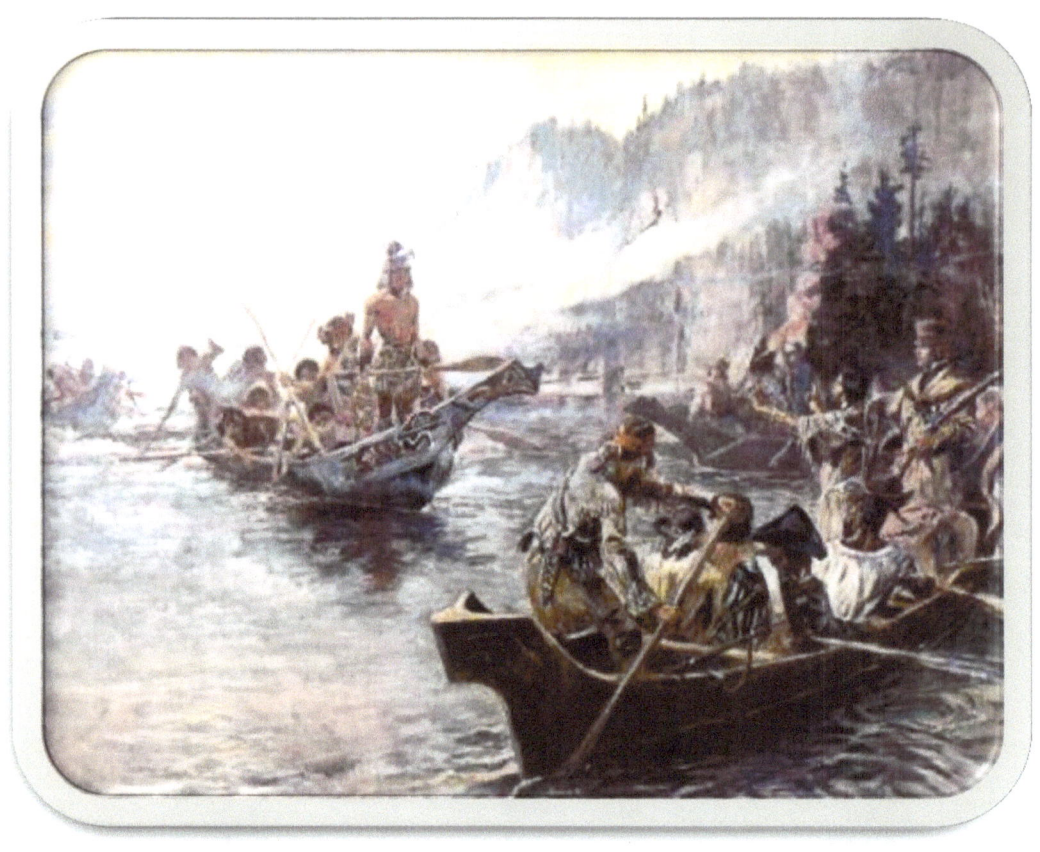

**Lewis and Clark
on the Lower Columbia
Charles Marion Russell, 1905
Lewis and Clark National
Historic Park**

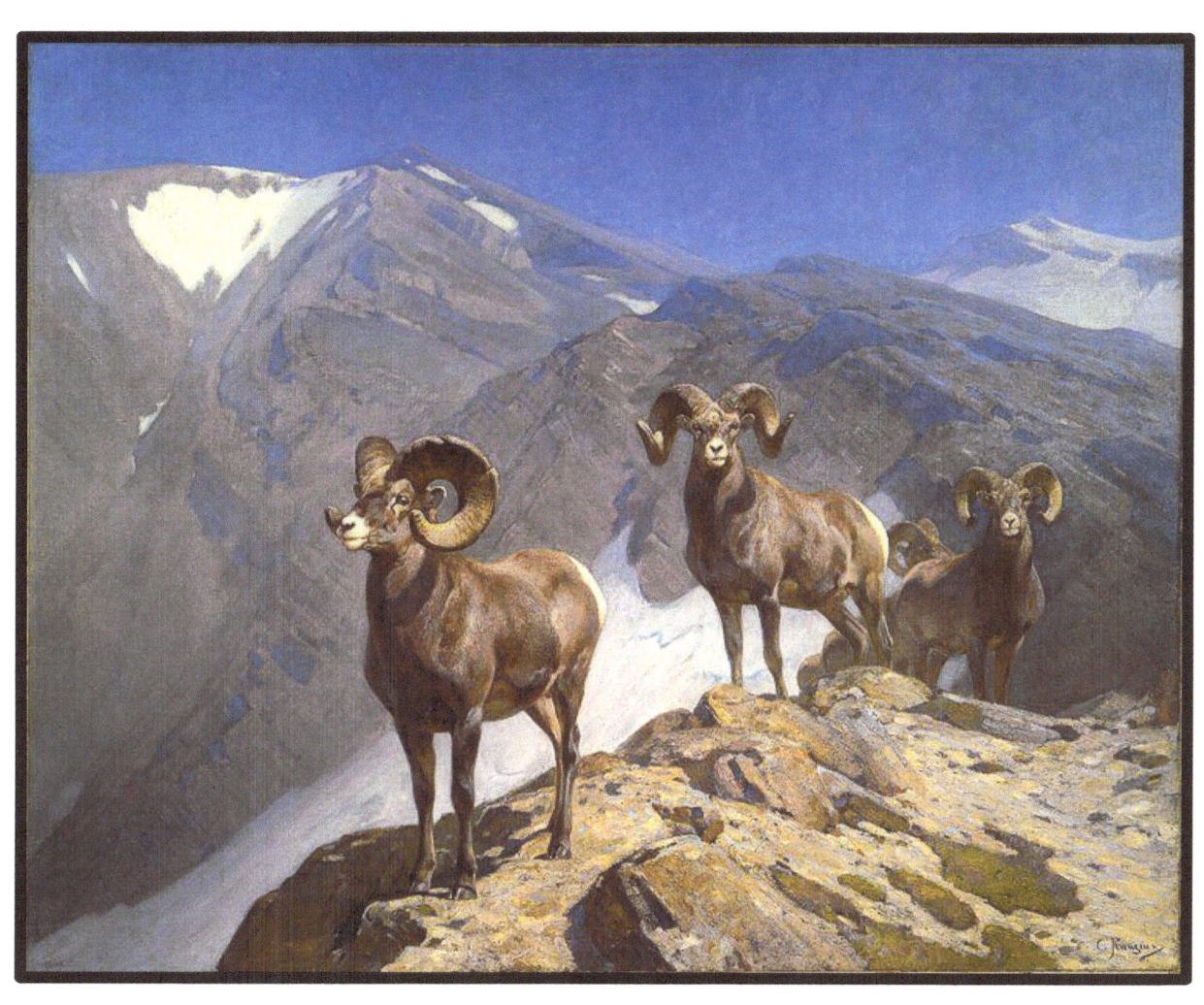

The Mountaineers

Carl Rungius, 1912

Canyonlands National Park

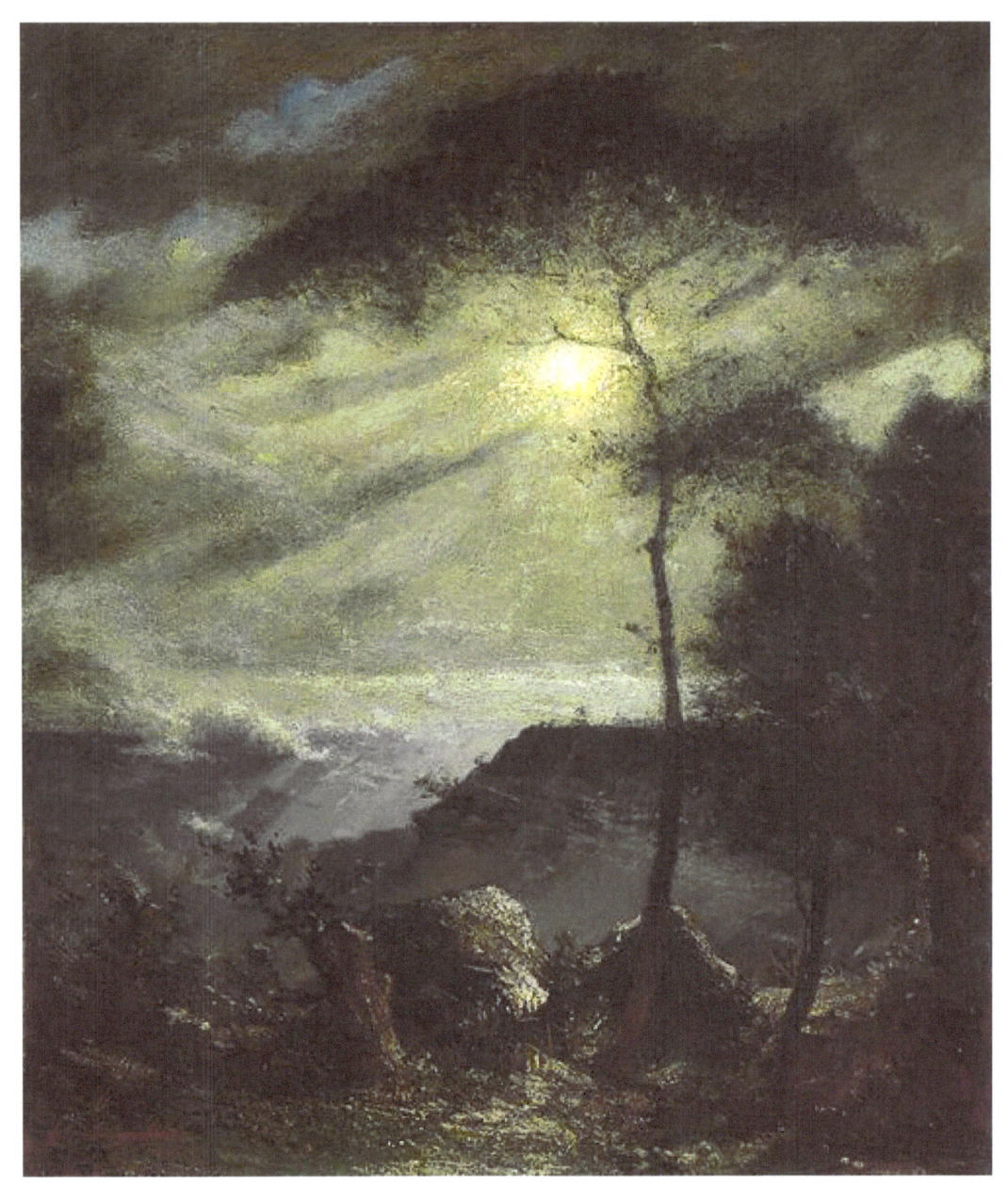

Above: Grand Canyon, Moonlight

Elliott Daingerfield, 1913

Grand Canyon National Park

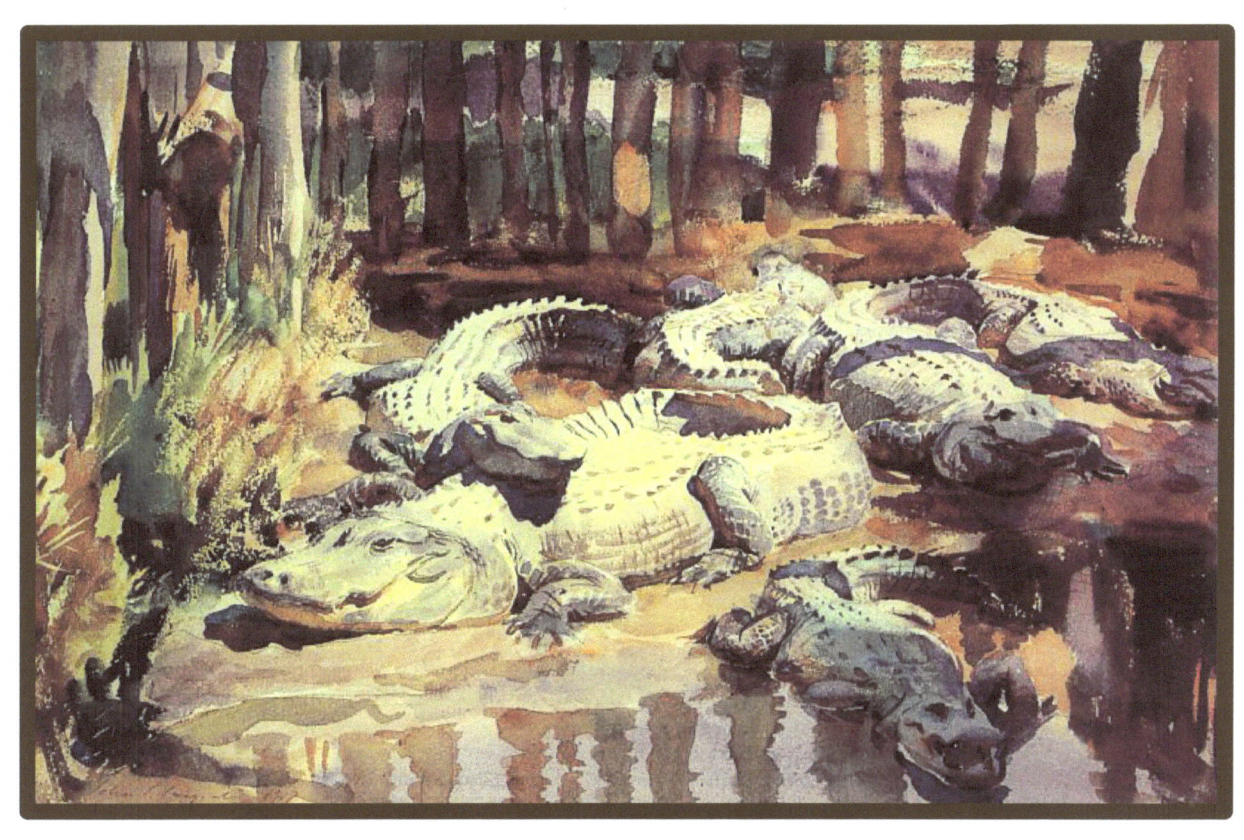

Below: Muddy Alligators

John Singer Sargent, 1917

Everglades National Park

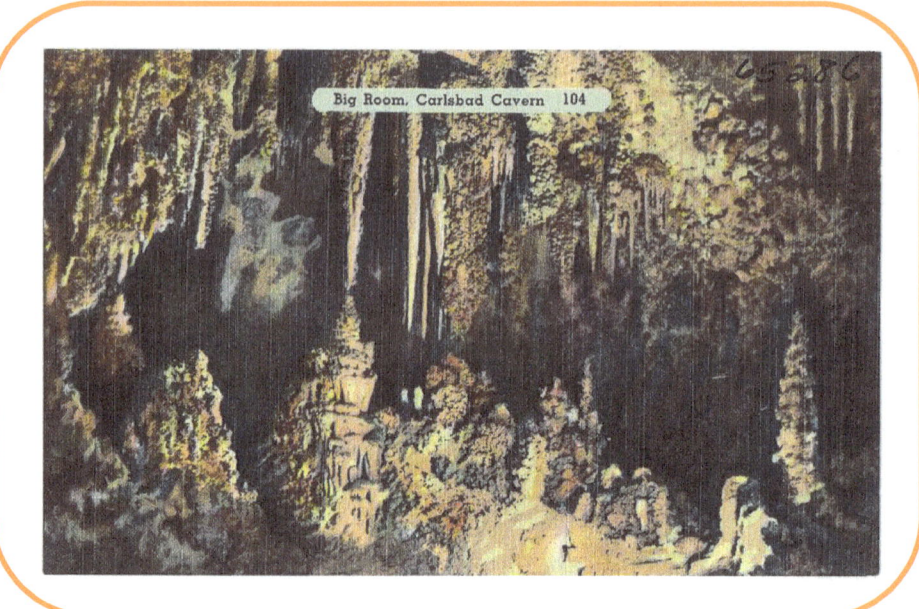

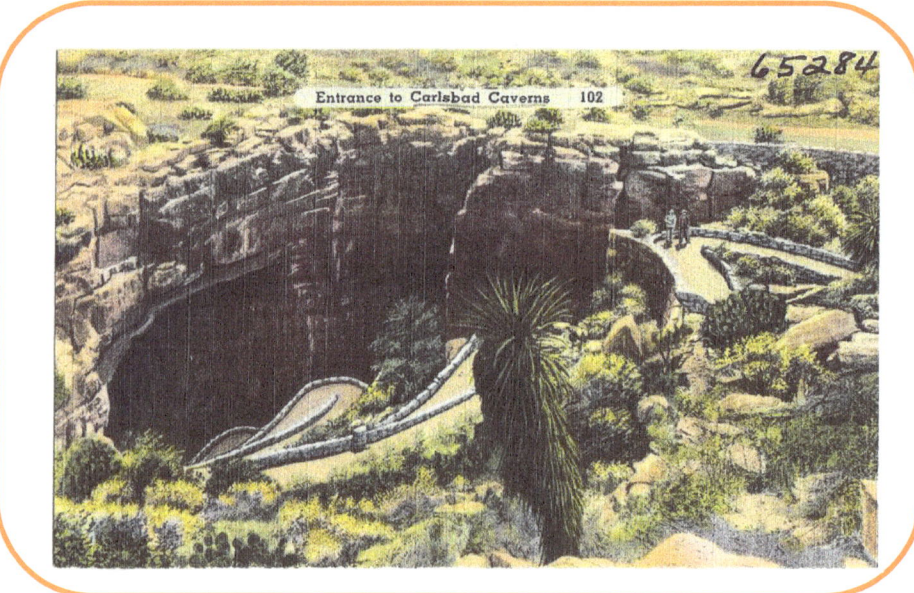

Upper- Big Room, Carlsbad Cavern

Lower- Entrance to Carlsbad Caverns

Both- National Park Service

circa 1930-1945

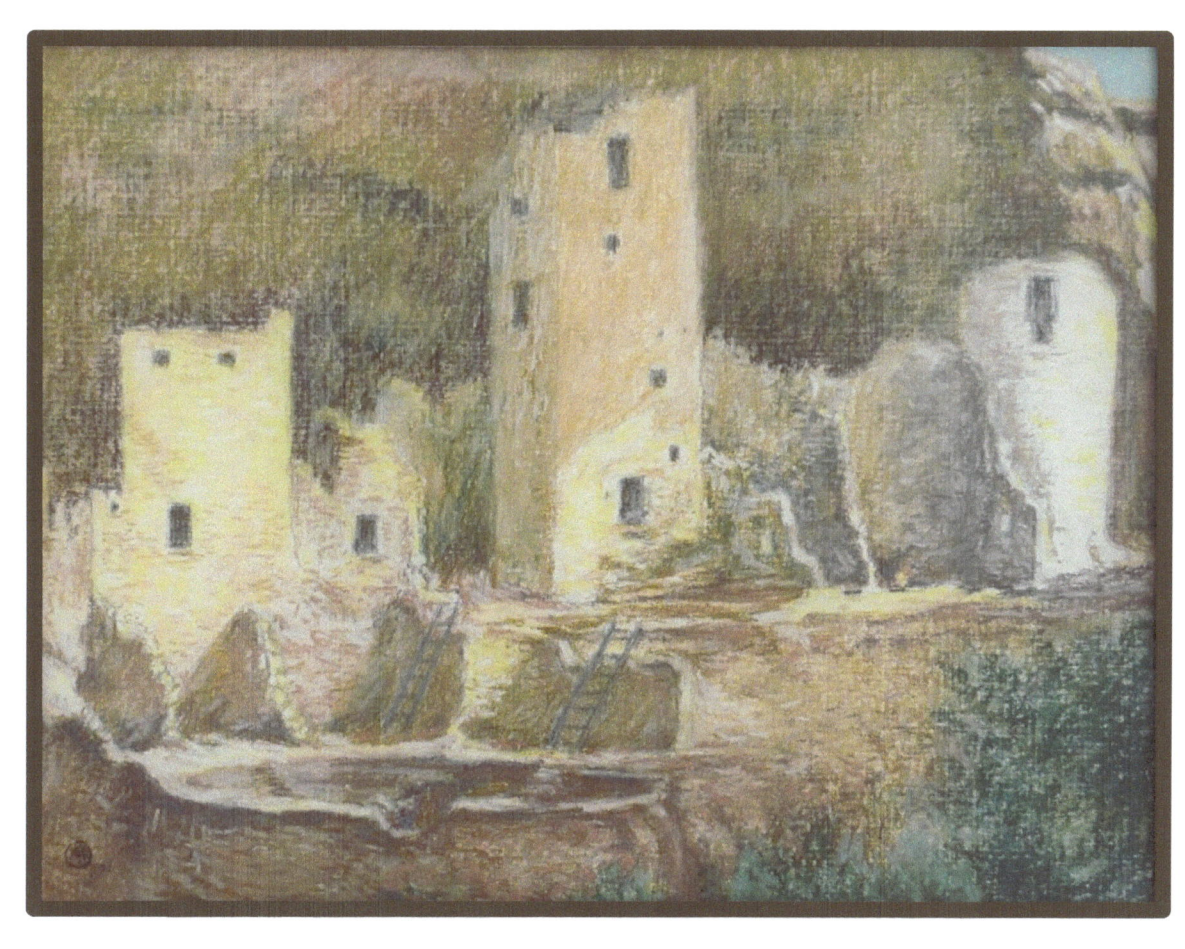

Cliff Palace

Mary Agnes Yerkes, 1973

Mesa Verde National Park

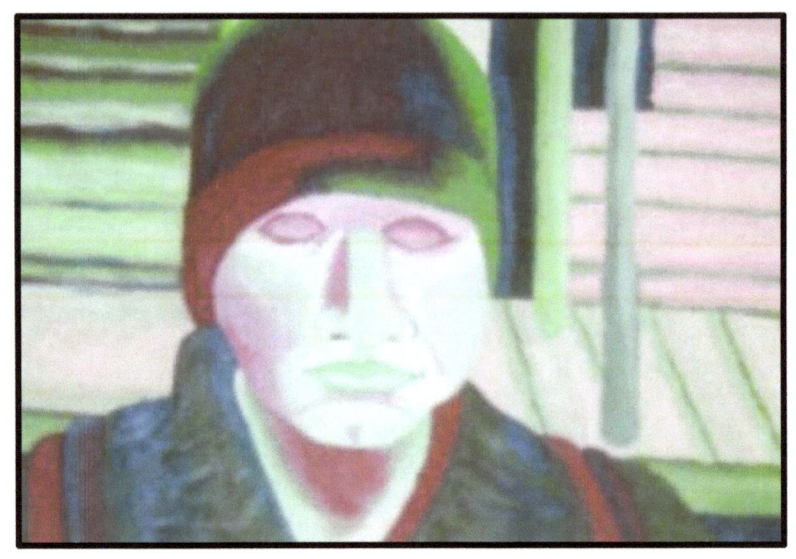

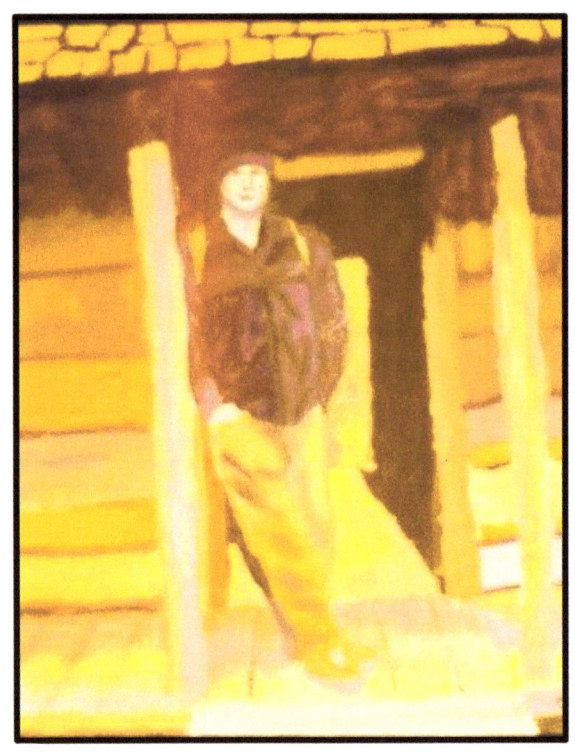

Above: In Thought

Below: Mountain Man

Both: Bonnie Hardison, 2003

Smokey Mountains National Park

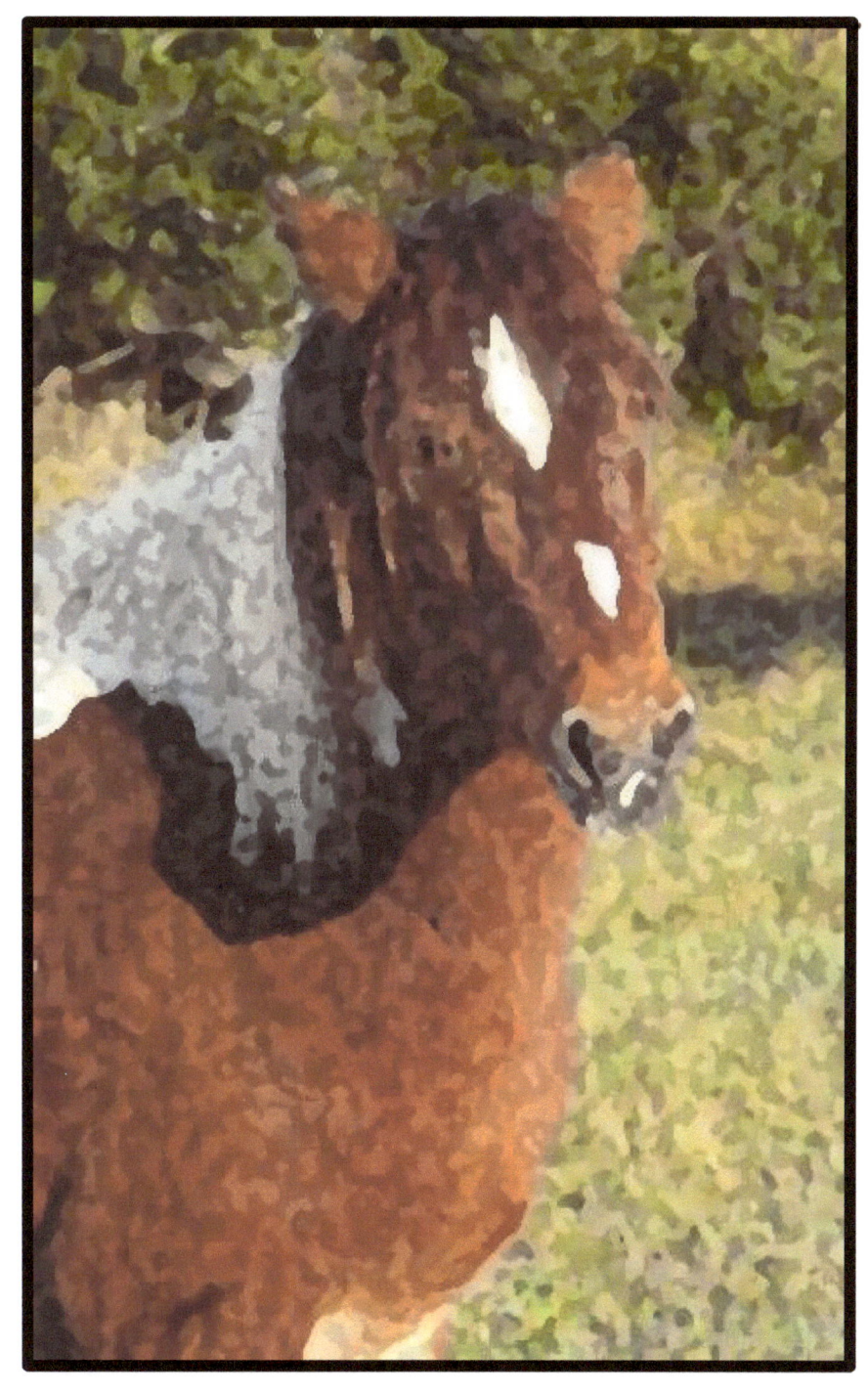

Chance, the Atlas of Assateague

Deirdre Fuller, 2008

Assateague National Seashore

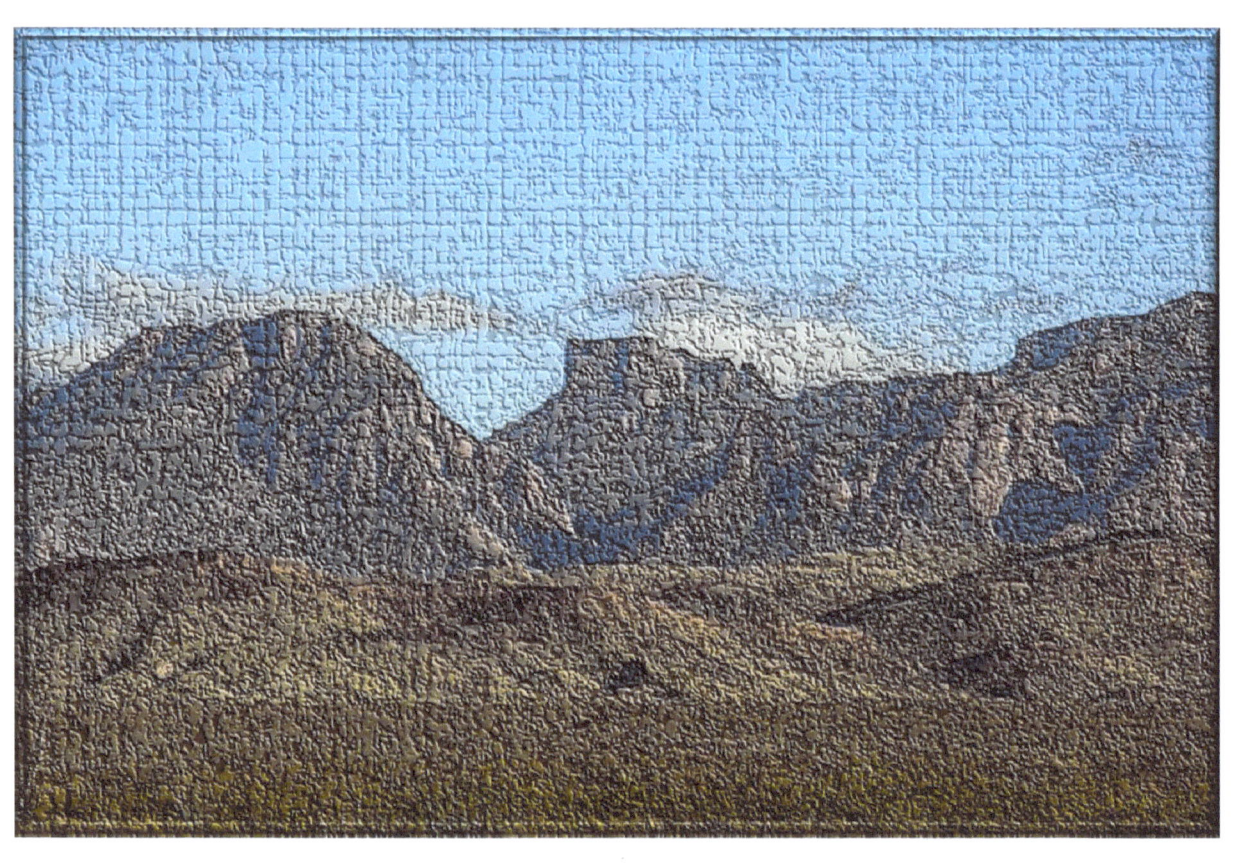

Casa Grande, A Different View

Robert Fuller, 2010

Big Bend National Park

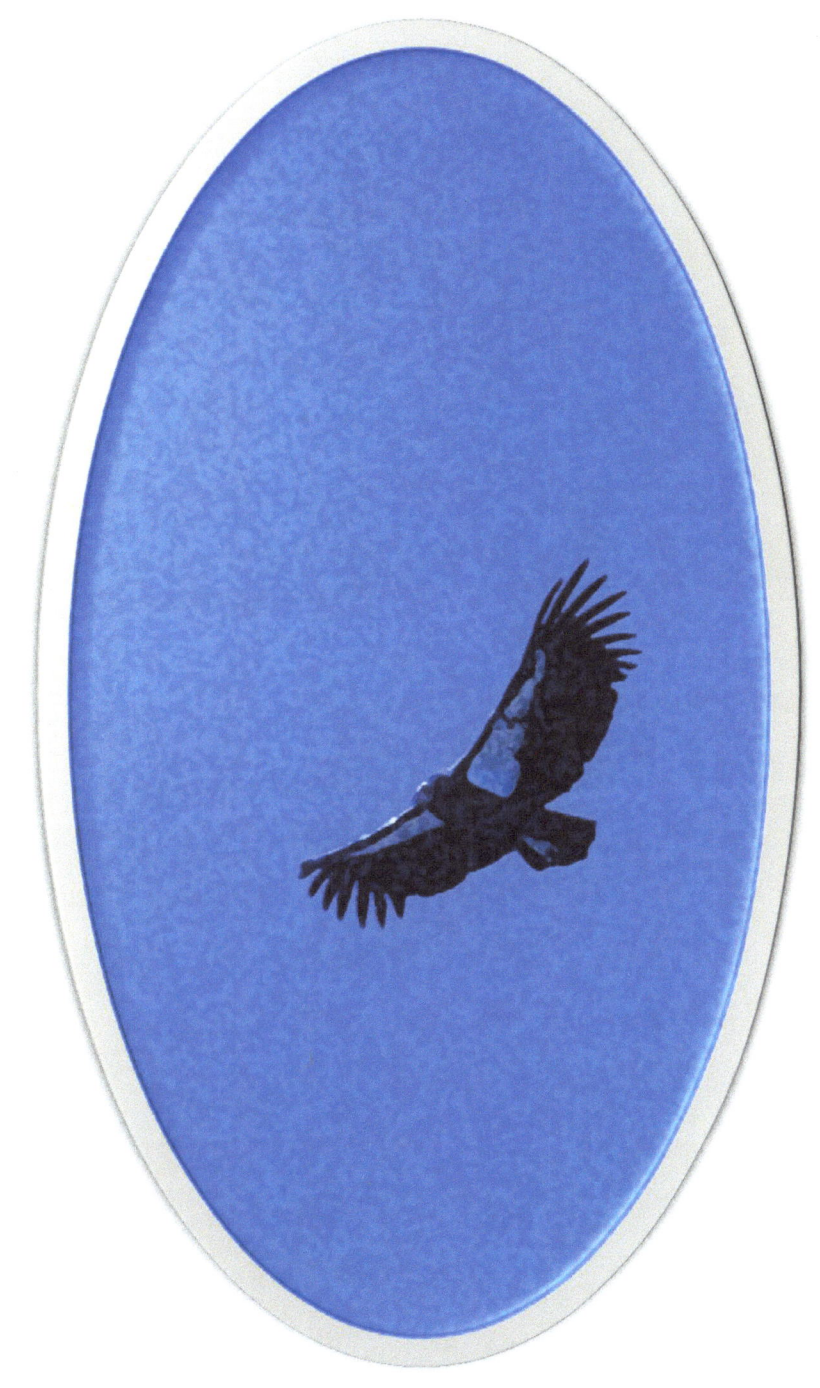

Condor in Flight

Robert Fuller, 2010

Pinnacles National Park

www.ingramcontent.com/pod-product-compliance
Lightning Source LLC
Chambersburg PA
CBHW050359180526
45159CB00005B/2079